Paper Folding
Made Easy

KRIS MASON

Published by

krause publications

700 East State Street • Iola, WI 54990-0001
715/445-2214 • FAX: 715/445-4087   www.krause.com

Please call or write for our free catalog of publications. Our toll-free number to place an order or obtain a free catalog is 800-258-0929, or please use our regular business telephone 715-445-2214.

Library of Congress Catalog Number: 2002105109

ISBN: 0-87349-451-2

Acknowledgments

For me, as an author, writing this book was like a journey through uncharted waters. There were rough times and times of smooth sailing. A great deal of recognition is owed to those who helped me stay the course. I would like to take this opportunity to acknowledge those who contributed their time, energy, and resources to this project. My sincere thanks go out to my Mom Pat, my sister Karie, and my friend Gina, for their suggestions and insight; my friends Melissa, and T. J. who braved the first drafts of folding instructions and helped me once and for all identify my right from my left; my friends Leslie and Sheila for contributing great photos to scrapbook and a willing ear.

For their unwavering love, support, and encouragement, I am eternally thankful to my husband Steve and kids Garrett and Marissa.

Special thanks also goes out to the staff at Krause, in particular Amy Tincher-Durik who was responsible for preparing the way for this project, Bob Best for taking the hundreds of beautiful photos for the book, and my terrific editor Jodi Rintelman (who found herself so entrenched in the experience that she admits to folding her candy wrappers) without whose help I would have surely drowned. This journey was successful due to the contributions of many people, and to them I extend my heartfelt thanks.

I would be remiss if I did not offer my greatest thanks to God for his faithfulness and for the talents and gifts he has given us all.

Contents

Sisters. Spruce up a basic mat or frame with a few folded rosebuds (page 90). You can wrap them up to look like a bouquet.

Introduction

Paper folding crafts have a rich history but are often thought to be too labor intensive and time consuming. With this book, I hope to change that view. As a passionate crafter and busy mother of two, I fell in love with the idea of a craft that was simple, portable, and required few tools yet possessed beauty and function. Paper folding fits the bill. I can take it with me anywhere, folding while I wait at soccer, ballet, swimming lessons, or the doctor. You name it. Then, when I have time to craft, the pieces are ready to go and all I have left to do is assemble my masterpiece. I was sold. The only drawback I found was that much of the available paper folding information seemed rather complicated. My theory is: Why make things harder than they need to be? Based on that theory, our journey begins.

With today's busy crafter in mind, I have set out to simplify the folding process and demonstrate the versatility of paper folding crafts. In this book you'll discover a variety of projects ranging from greeting cards to home décor. All are designed for beginners to achieve great results with no prior knowledge of folding necessary. Using these simple folding techniques, you'll soon impress your friends with handmade folded craft projects.

To help you get started, you'll find eight sheets of Folded Memories® patterned folding paper included in this book! Knowledge of some basic craft techniques will be helpful but not essential. Most projects involve cutting, folding, and gluing; some will incorporate other familiar craft techniques like stamping, punching, and matting.

Chapter 1 Getting Started

A BRIEF HISTORY

Paper folding is a centuries old art form that has universal appeal. Its enthusiasts span the globe and are limited to no particular demographic. Whether folding gum wrappers, teabags, or fine handmade papers, people young and old are enjoying the art of paper folding.

Historically speaking, paper folding can be traced to an ancient Japanese tradition, commonly known as origami. Most origami techniques use a single sheet of paper cleverly folded to create a three-dimensional object such as a boat or swan. These objects are created for the joy and challenge of the process rather than a practical use of the finished project. Although origami is still alive and well in the twenty-first century, it has undergone many transformations. Modern day crafters have begun to take the principals of origami and adapt them to conform to their crafting arena.

This process first emerged in Europe in the late 1990s as a flat, multi-piece form of origami known as Teabag Folding. As the story goes, a Dutch woman pondered the need to make a card for an upcoming birthday while sipping a cup of tea. The paper envelope that the tea bag was packaged in had a beautiful drawing on it. Inspired, she set out to cut and fold the tea wrapper into an embellishment for her card. Since the tea wrapper was quite small, more were needed to accomplish the task. When she was done, she discovered that when you start each fold with the same picture in the same place and combine them together the result is a folded medal-

lion with a kaleidoscope effect. The beauty of this one creation sparked a craft trend that had card makers across Europe raiding their pantries for teabag folding supplies. Lucky for us, manufactures caught on and began producing square pattern paper for the craft.

Once teabag folding hit the United States, it did not take long for scrapbook enthusiasts like myself to recognize the potential for scrapbook embellishment. Through the development of folded frames and borders, *Memory Folding*™ emerged. Today paper folding crafts are among the craft industry's hottest trends.

Beyond its obvious creative appeal, paper folding has several other benefits. Many teachers use paper folding in the classroom to teach children math concepts and to develop small motor skills. Physical therapists have used folding to aid in recovery from hand injuries and other hand and wrist-related conditions. More than anything else, paper folding is just plain FUN.

With *fun* being the operative word, I have set out to create this book to share with you my own interpretation of the art of paper folding. These projects are designed to be fun and easy as well as useful. Recreate the projects exactly as you see them or use them as a springboard and adapt them to your own crafting style. I will offer suggestions along the way for other uses or variations. Enjoy!

Kris

Here's a fun variation on the Bug Box (page 74) topped with the Diamond Fold (page 28).

PAPER POSSIBILITIES

Paper is one of the most abundant resources in the craft world. Craft, stamp, and scrapbook stores now carry a wide variety of paper products. Some cities are lucky enough to have stores that carry nothing but paper! For those of you who don't have local resources available, the Internet has made even unique and specialty papers as close as a click away. Check the resource guide at the back of the book for a list of my favorite sites.

Paper is the primary component for the projects in this book, so lets take a look at some of the different types of paper and their uses in regard to folding.

BACKGROUND PAPER

Solid or printed light-weight paper is commonly called background paper. This type of paper is widely available. It's usually found in sizes 8½" x 11" or 12" x 12". A variety of color combinations and themes are available. This paper folds well and can be cut into squares of many different sizes to suite your specific project needs.

CARDSTOCK

Cardstock, also known as cover stock, is heavier in weight and therefore stiffer to fold. Available in matte and glossy finishes, it's best used in larger projects like boxes or home décor. Cardstock is available in many colors, some with subtle patterns such as speckle or marbling.

TEXTURED PAPER

There are many types of textured papers available in both light and heavy weights. Some examples of textured papers are:

Suede: Soft and fuzzy-feeling material with a light paper backing. This paper doesn't hold a crease as well as some other types, but it can add a rich effect to the finished project. Working with this medium is a little more time consuming, but the results are worth the extra effort.

Embossed: Medium to heavy-weight paper with raised designs. In most cases, embossed paper is easy to fold. The raised images give added dimension to your folded elements.

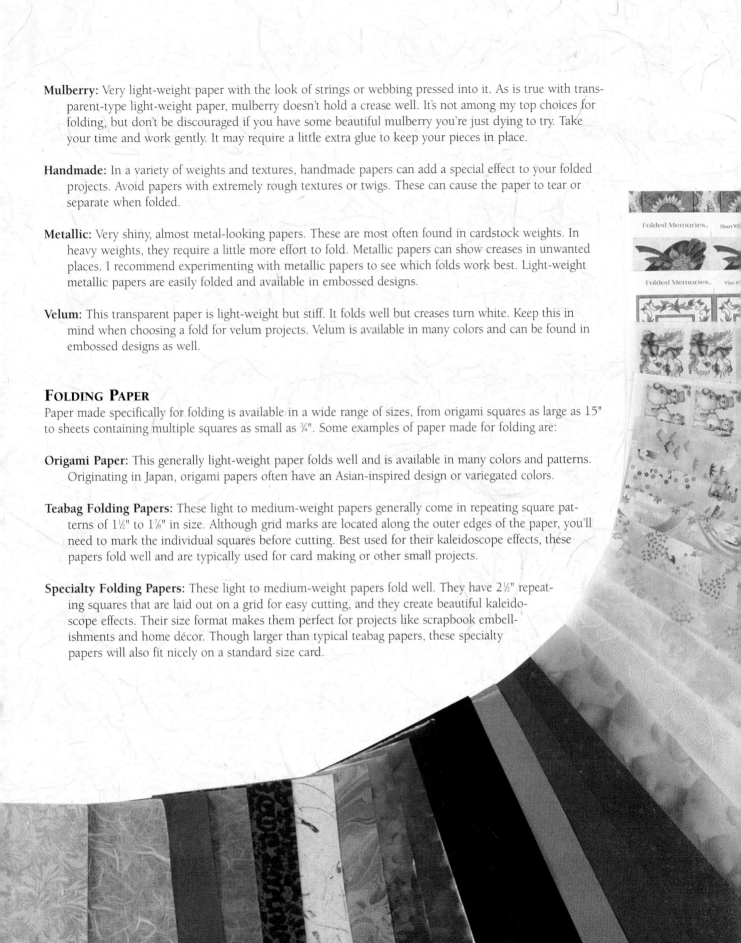

Mulberry: Very light-weight paper with the look of strings or webbing pressed into it. As is true with transparent-type light-weight paper, mulberry doesn't hold a crease well. It's not among my top choices for folding, but don't be discouraged if you have some beautiful mulberry you're just dying to try. Take your time and work gently. It may require a little extra glue to keep your pieces in place.

Handmade: In a variety of weights and textures, handmade papers can add a special effect to your folded projects. Avoid papers with extremely rough textures or twigs. These can cause the paper to tear or separate when folded.

Metallic: Very shiny, almost metal-looking papers. These are most often found in cardstock weights. In heavy weights, they require a little more effort to fold. Metallic papers can show creases in unwanted places. I recommend experimenting with metallic papers to see which folds work best. Light-weight metallic papers are easily folded and available in embossed designs.

Velum: This transparent paper is light-weight but stiff. It folds well but creases turn white. Keep this in mind when choosing a fold for velum projects. Velum is available in many colors and can be found in embossed designs as well.

FOLDING PAPER

Paper made specifically for folding is available in a wide range of sizes, from origami squares as large as 15" to sheets containing multiple squares as small as ¾". Some examples of paper made for folding are:

Origami Paper: This generally light-weight paper folds well and is available in many colors and patterns. Originating in Japan, origami papers often have an Asian-inspired design or variegated colors.

Teabag Folding Papers: These light to medium-weight papers generally come in repeating square patterns of 1½" to 1⅞" in size. Although grid marks are located along the outer edges of the paper, you'll need to mark the individual squares before cutting. Best used for their kaleidoscope effects, these papers fold well and are typically used for card making or other small projects.

Specialty Folding Papers: These light to medium-weight papers fold well. They have 2½" repeating squares that are laid out on a grid for easy cutting, and they create beautiful kaleidoscope effects. Their size format makes them perfect for projects like scrapbook embellishments and home décor. Though larger than typical teabag papers, these specialty papers will also fit nicely on a standard size card.

A Few Paper Tips

* If you're creating a project for scrapbooking, be sure to use papers and adhesives that are identified as archival quality.

* Because most folding squares are 3" or smaller, paper folding is a great way to make use of your scraps and leftovers from other paper projects.

* You can create your own paper designs by using techniques like stamping or sponging.

* Get creative and experiment with folding different materials, such as doilies, paper lace, or even fabrics.

Tools and Basic Necessities

Most projects can be made with common craft tools. The supply list given with each project will identify specific supply needs.

Here is a list of common tools that will be helpful when creating your folded projects:

* Long ruler, 15" or longer

* Scissors (regular and decorative)

* Pencil

* Liquid adhesive (I like Delta's Archival Quality Photo Safe Glue. It is pliable and dries quickly. If this product isn't available in your area, any liquid clear-drying glue will work.)

* Double sided tape or photo mount tabs

* Boning tool

* Paper cutter (My favorite is the X-Acto® rotary paper trimmer, produced by Hunt Corporation. It's the only one I've found with the blade running against a metal edge so you can count on a straight cut even when working with several pages at a time.)

UNDERSTANDING THE INSTRUCTIONS

When beginning a project, first check the supply list for any additional items you may need to assist in completing your project. Once you have gathered your supplies, you're ready to begin.

All of the folding instructions are designed to be user-friendly. Step-by-step photos accompanied by written instructions will guide you through the process. Each photo will show what the piece should look like when the written instruction for that step is complete. In some cases, the photo will show both the motion of the fold and the finished form. These photos help you see where the fold starts and ends in a single glance.

The photo instructions are shot from what I like to call an "over my shoulder "perspective. What this means is, what you see in the photo should match what is in front of you, as if you were watching from over my shoulder.

My right is your right, my left is your left, and so on. Some of the instructions will also have symbols to help guide you. The symbols and their meanings can be found in the following Tips and Terminology section. Using the written instructions, combined with the aid of photos and symbols, you'll complete your folded projects like an old pro.

TIPS AND TERMINOLOGY

TIPS

Here are a few tips to help you along the way:

* Start simple. Although all of the projects in this book are designed with beginners in mind, make your first project a simple one with only five or six steps. You'll find several to choose from.

* Don't be in a hurry. Take your time and read the instructions through before you begin.

* Be precise. Sloppy folding can result in things not lining up the way they should in the end.

* Crease well. Sharp creases make for better-looking finished projects.

* Squares are square. A square by definition is equal on all sides, so take care in cutting your folding squares. The more exact the square, the better the finished piece.

* Practice makes perfect. When trying a fold for the first time, use scrap paper to get familiar with the fold before breaking out the good stuff.

* Use liquid glue in moderation. When assembling your folded elements, use glue sparingly. You can always add more if needed. If you use too much glue it will ooze out the flaps and, trust me that is messy. Also, make sure to cap your liquid adhesive between steps (or keep a stick pin handy).

* Have fun.

SYMBOLS

A fold or crease line toward you.

A fold or crease line away from you.

Flip over

Direction

Point of reference

TERMINOLOGY
Specific to folding

Folded piece: This refers to a single folded piece of paper yet to be assembled into a folded element.

Folded element: The finished form of several folded pieces artfully combined together.

Assembly: The process of combining any given number of folded pieces into a folded element.

Flap: A movable component of a folded piece.

General craft

Mounting: The process of attaching one piece to another with two-sided tape or other adhesive.

Mounting Tape: Small pre-cut strips of two-sided tape (also referred to as photo tabs).

Foam Mounting Tape: Two sided tape or tabs with foam in between to create a dimensional effect.

Matting: The process of creating an additional outer edge or frame on a finished element, photo, or other project component. Matting adds dimension and definition to the piece.

Cropping: The process of cutting paper or photos to a specific shape or size.

Journaling: Handwritten or computer generated text that tells the story or identifies specific information about a person or event. You'll most often find journaling in scrapbook projects.

Wrong side: The plain or backside of the paper.

Right side: As in "the right side facing up," is the printed or front side of the paper.

DISCOVERING REPETITIVE PATTERNS

Example 1A

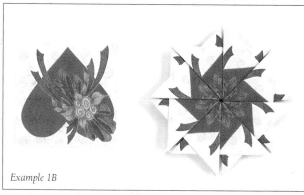

Example 1B

Repetitive patterns work to further enhance the techniques you'll learn in this book by allowing you to use the same folding instructions to create distinctively differently results. When working with the same image on each square (rather than solid colored or a random pattern squares), each individual illustration provides the choice of at least four different repetitive patterns. Those options change depending on the fold and assembly you choose. Pattern changes also occur when changing a fold from left to right or right to left. Once you've learned the basics of folding, you'll be ready to explore this next level of design.

So, what exactly are repetitive patterns?

Repetitive patterns are the added design or kaleido-scope effects you get when you begin the folding process with the same image on each square. Any given image on a square has the ability to develop into several different repetitive patterns. The repeating patterns change, depending on how you view the square before you begin. Let me demonstrate for you. In the following example each element was made with the same fold and the same paper. The finished effects are quite different!

Example #1A uses the Heart patterned paper with the heart to the top, as you would normally view it.

Example #2A uses the Heart patterned paper turned upside down with the point to the top.

Example 2A

Example 2B

As you can see, changing the direction of the pattern on the square changes the end result as well.

Here are the same examples, showing the change you get when using an open assembly (an element with an opening in the center to house a photograph) rather than a closed assembly (one with no opening in the center).

Example #1B uses the Heart patterned paper with the heart to the top, as you would normally view it.

Example #2B uses the Heart patterned paper turned upside down with the point to the top.

The key to repetitive patterns is consistency. All squares must show the same image viewed in the same direction.

Each of the projects in this book, using repetitive patterns, will identify how to orient the image to accomplish the look in the featured project. Now that you know how to change patterns, you can play around with these projects and create different looks with the same paper and instructions. If you feel creative, experiment and have fun. You'll be amazed at the outcome.

Chapter 2

Cards

1. Happy Birthday
page 12

2. Vine
page 14

3. Fishing
page 16

4. Thinking of You
page 18

5. Metallic
page 20

6. Baby
page 22

7. Journal and Pen Set
page 24

8. Kitty
page 26

9. Joy
page 28

10. Make Your Own Envelopes
page 30

Happy Birthday (watercolor)

This watercolor look is proof positive that repetitive patterns are not necessary to create appealing effects. Complimented by the subtle movement of colors, the Turn-Style fold adds dimension and a feel of motion to this custom made birthday card.

TECHNIQUE

Turn-style Fold

SUPPLIES

For folding

- 1 sheet watercolor squares paper[1] (cut eight 2" squares; save the remainder)

- Liquid adhesive[2]

For card

- 1 sheet lime green cardstock (cut one 5½" x 8½" rectangle, fold in half; one 3" square)

- Remaining watercolor squares paper[1] (cut one 3¾" square)

- Happy Birthday stamp and ink

- Mounting tape, ruler, craft knife, scissors or paper cutter, pencil

In this project: [1]MM Colors by Design®, [2]Delta®.

Turn-Style Fold

Complete the following steps for each square:

1 Place the square face down, so that the wrong side is up.

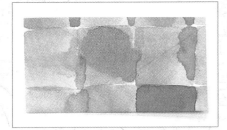

2 Fold the bottom edge up to the top.

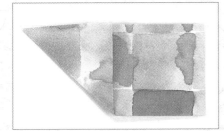

3 Fold the bottom left corner up to the top forming a small triangle flap.

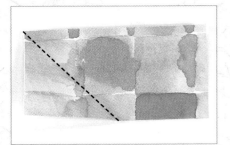

4 Fold the flap back to its original position.

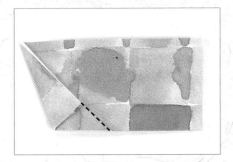

5 Fold the left edge over to meet the crease line.

6 Fold the flap up along the crease line.

Assembly

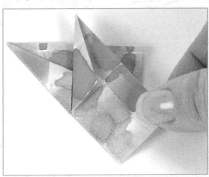

1 With the folded piece positioned horizontally, place a small amount of adhesive on the lower right side of one piece.

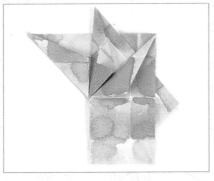

2 Place the next piece on top of the first, so that the long folded edge of the top piece meets the short folded edge of the bottom piece and the bottom points meet.

3 When adding the third piece, you'll notice that its upper point will line up with the upper right corner of the first piece.

4 Continue adding pieces in this manner. The first piece will lie on top of the last.

Card assembly

1 Mount the folded element centered on the green square.

2 On the upper left corner of the watercolor paper, measure over 1" and down $\frac{7}{16}$". Make a faint pencil mark. Go back to the corner and measure down 1" and over $\frac{7}{16}$". Make a faint pencil mark. Using a ruler and craft knife, connect the pencil marks, and then make an identical slit $\frac{1}{16}$" away from the first slit. Repeat for the other three corners.
Slide the corners of the green square under the slits in the watercolor square. Secure with mounting tape.

3 With the folded edge of the card on the left, mount the watercolor square centered $\frac{1}{4}$" from the top.

4 Stamp your greeting in the space below the watercolor square.

Vine

The layering of geometric shapes makes this card unique. The diamond opening in the center allows for the option of inserting a separate note or stamped message. In this case, the open center adds a woven look. The Jacket Fold is one of only a few folds that can be assembled in a rectangle or a square shape.

TECHNIQUE

Jacket Fold

SUPPLIES

For folding

- 1 sheet Vine paper[1] (cut six 2½" squares)
- Liquid adhesive[2]

For card

- 1 sheet black cardstock (cut one 5½" x 8½" rectangle, fold in half; one 4" x 5½" rectangle)
- 1 sheet crème cardstock (crop to 4" x 5⅜")
- 1 sheet dark green cardstock (crop to 3⅞" x 5¼")
- Mounting tape, ruler, scissors or paper cutter

In this project: [1]Folded Memories®, [2]Delta.

Jacket Fold

Complete the following steps for four squares:

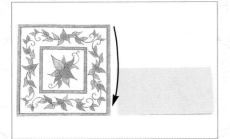

1 With the right side of the paper facing you (pattern as shown), fold the top edge down to the bottom edge.

2 Fold the top layer of the left corner up to the top folded edge to make a small triangle.

3 Repeat step #2 on the right corner.

4 Fold the bottom point up to the long folded edge, forming a small triangle.

Assembly

1 Hold one piece vertically with the folded edge to the left. Place a small amount of adhesive near the top right corner.

2 Hold the next piece horizontally with the folded edge to the top. Place the left edge of the horizontal piece in the space between the fold and flat back of the other piece, creating a right angle.

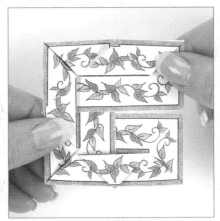

3 Repeat steps #1 and #2 with the third piece.

4 The last piece slides between the first and the third pieces so that one end goes on top of #3's back flap and the other goes behind #1's back flap to create a square.

5 Hold your finished piece like a diamond. Matt the right side point with a flat vine square, lining up the point with the inside square in the paper design. Secure with adhesive, and repeat on the left side.

Card Assembly

1 Mount the crème rectangle centered on one side of the folded black rectangle.

2 Mount the green rectangle centered on the crème rectangle.

3 Mount the folded element centered on the other black rectangle. Trim the excess so that the element has a 1/16" border around all sides.

4 Mount the bordered element to the center of the card.

Fishing

Good masculine cards can be hard to come by. This card creates a masculine feel with the combination of dark rich colors and the fishing motif. To customize this card, you can certainly change the Dad stamp to read Son or a specific name. Not a stamper? No problem. For an interesting alternative, try turning the card on its side (fold at the top) and hang the fish in the space previously occupied by the stamp. Because of the use of a real fishhook, I recommend this card for hand delivery. If you must post it, use a padded envelope and boldly mark HAND CANCEL on the outside.

TECHNIQUE

Arrowhead Fold

SUPPLIES

For folding
- 12" x 12" sheet Napoleon Marble Gold paper[1] (cut eight 2" squares; save the remainder)
- Liquid adhesive[2]

For card
- 12" x 12" sheet Marquina Marble Gold paper[1] (cut one 3¼" diameter circle)

- Remaining Napoleon Marble Gold paper[1] (cut one 3¾" x 5" rectangle)
- 2 sheets brown cardstock (cut one 3½" diameter circle; one 8½" x 5½" rectangle, fold in half; save the remainder)
- Notch corner punch[3]
- Pop Dots™ (foam tabs) adhesive[4]
- Fishhook[5]
- Fish die cut[6]
- Dad stamp[7] and ink
- 5" length of thread
- Circle cutter or template
- Ruler, scissors or paper cutter

In this project: [1]Scrap-Ease®, [2]Delta, [3]Carl®, [4]All Night Media®, [5]Crystal River®, [6]Bumper Crops®, [7]Inkadinkado®.

ARROWHEAD FOLD

Complete the following steps for each square:

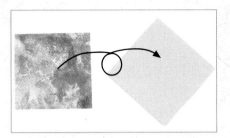

1 Place the square right side up. Flip the stack over and rotate to look like a diamond.

2 Fold the bottom point up to make a triangle.

3 Fold the left point over to the right point and crease well.

4 Fold the top flap on the right side over and down to line up with the folded edge on the left.

ASSEMBLY

1 Place one arrowhead piece so that the bottom right edge is horizontal and the upper point is at about 11 o'clock. Place a small amount of adhesive on the right point.

2 Lift up the flap on the left. Pick up the next piece, and hold it opposite to the first so that the left edge is horizontal and the upper point is at 1 o'clock.

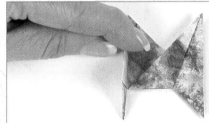

3 Lay piece #2 on top of piece #1 so that the left point meets the raised flap and the bottom edges line up.

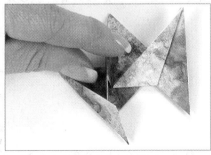

4 Rotate the pieces so that piece #2 is now in the #1 position, and then add the next piece as above. Continue in this manner with all pieces.

5 To finish, piece #1 slides inside piece #8 to complete the pattern.

CARD ASSEMBLY

1 Punch all four corners of the 3¾" x 5" Napoleon Marble Gold rectangle with the notch punch.

2 Mount the rectangle centered on the brown card. The fold of the card should be at the left.

3 Mount the Marquina Marble Gold circle centered on the brown circle.

4 Mount the brown circle centered ¼" from the top of the matting on the card.

5 Stamp Dad on the lower right of the card.

6 Mount the folded element to the remaining brown paper. Trim the excess, leaving a ⅛" border.

7 Using the Pop Dots, mount the folded element to the center of the Marquina Marble Gold circle.

8 Cut out the fish die, and hang it from the fishhook.

9 Run thread through the end of the fishhook and tie a slipknot about ¾" up. Trim off the excess.

10 Hang the fishhook, by the loop in the slipknot, from the upper left point of the folded element. Secure with adhesive from behind.

4 Thinking of You (flower trio)

Much like the Diamond Fold, the Triangle Fold is what I like to call a Mother Fold. From this base, simply adding a few new steps can create many different finished shapes and effects. Once you're familiar with the Triangle Fold, you'll easily master many other folds found in this book.

TECHNIQUE

Triangle Fold

SUPPLIES

For folding
- 1 sheet Flower Trio paper[1] (cut eight 2½" squares)
- Liquid adhesive[2]

For card
- 2 sheets purple paper (cut one 7½" x 8" rectangle, fold in half to 3¾" x 8"; one 3¾" diameter circle)

- 1 sheet white cardstock (cut one 7" x 3¼" rectangle; trim two ¼" sections off of the 7" length and save the pieces)
- 1 sheet green paper (cut one 3" diameter circle)
- Pop Dots (foam tabs) adhesive[3]
- Thinking Of You stamp and Ink
- Circle cutter or templates
- Mounting tape
- Ruler, scissors or paper cutter

In this project: [1]Folded Memories paper provided in the middle of the book, [2]Delta, [3]All Night Media.

TRIANGLE FOLD

Complete the following steps for each square:

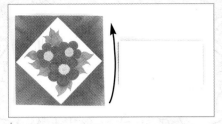

1 With the pattern side facing up, fold the bottom edge up to the top edge, making a rectangle.

2 Open the piece flat, fold the left side over to the right.

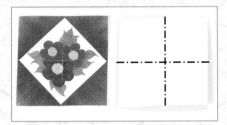

3 Open the piece flat, flip the paper over (wrong side is now facing you).

4 Fold the upper left corner down to the lower right corner to form a triangle.

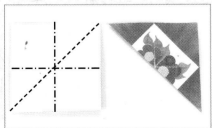

5 Open the piece flat. Fold the lower left corner up to the upper right corner.

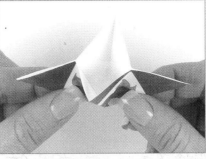

6 Pick up the piece with the folded edge at the bottom. Holding along the outer points of the folded edge, with both hands, push thumbs up and toward the center, forming star.

7 Press flat to from a layered triangle. There will be two flaps on the left and two flaps on the right.

ASSEMBLY

1 Rotate the flaps of your finished pieces until all eight pieces show this image.

2 Pick piece #1 with the closed point at the bottom. Slightly open the flaps on the right side, and place a small amount of adhesive in the crease.

3 With your other hand, pick up piece #2. Place the top left flap of piece #2 between the two triangle flaps on the right side of piece #1. Slide the pieces together until they stop and the bottom points meet.

4 Continue adding pieces in this manner.

5 After adding piece #8, bring the flaps of piece #1 forward and into piece #8 to properly continue the pattern. There may be a small hole in the center. Add additional adhesive as necessary.

CARD ASSEMBLY

1 Mount the white rectangle centered on the card. Mount the ¼" white strips centered above and below the white rectangle.

2 Mount the folded element centered on the green circle.

3 Mount the green circle centered on the purple circle.

4 Mount the purple circle centered about ¼" down from the top of the white rectangle.

5 Stamp the message centered below the folded element.

Metallic

This oversized square card has a dramatic effect. The combination of metallic and embossed papers gives it a shimmering quality. Remember that square cards require extra postage to send through the mail. If a square or odd-size envelope is in order, check out the Make Your Own Envelope project on page 30.

TECHNIQUE

Single Stair Fold

SUPPLIES

For folding

- 2 sheets silver metallic paper[1] (cut eight 3" squares)
- Liquid adhesive[2]

For card

- 1 sheet 12" x 12" black with gold embossed leaf paper[3] (crop to 6" x 12", fold in half)
- 1 sheet black cardstock (cut one 4" square; one 5" square)
- Silver metallic pen
- Mounting tape
- Ruler, craft knife, scissors or paper cutter

In this project: [1]Kolubki Trading Co., [2]Delta, [3]Robins Nest Press.

SINGLE STAIR FOLD

Follow steps #1–6 of the Triangle Fold (page18) for each square, followed by:

1 With the closed point down, fold the right top flap over to the left. There should be three flaps on the left and one on the right.

2 Fold the left top flap down to the center crease.

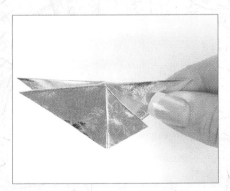

3 Bring the small folded flap (the stair) from the left over to the right.

ASSEMBLY

Note: The metallic papers cause the adhesive to dry slowly. Take your time on this assembly.

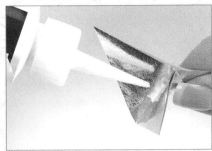

1 With your right hand, pick up piece #1 with the closed point at the bottom. Open the flaps on the left, and place a small amount of adhesive on the right back flap.

2 With your other hand, pick up piece #2. Place the single flap of piece #1 in between the two triangle flaps on the left side of piece #2. Slide the pieces together until they stop and the bottom points meet. The small folded triangle should remain on the top.

3 Continue adding pieces in this manner.

4 Piece #1 will sit inside piece #8 to complete the pattern. There may be a small hole in the center. Add additional adhesive as necessary.

CARD ASSEMBLY

1 To make the frame, cut a 4½" square out of the center of the 5" black square. Use a ruler and metallic pen to draw a line, centered lengthwise, through each side of the frame.

2 Mount the frame centered on the card.

3 Mount the 4" black square centered, like a diamond, over the frame.

4 Mount the folded element centered on the black square.

Baby

Whether you're announcing a birth or congratulating the parents of a newborn, this card is just the ticket. Make it in blue for a boy, pink for a girl, or combine pink and blue if the lucky couple had one of each. This special card is one that's sure to end up in baby's book to keep.

To make the ball ornament in the background, see page 68 and substitute Berry Sponge paper.

TECHNIQUE

V-wing Fold

SUPPLIES

For folding
- 1 sheet 12" x 12" hand and foot print paper[1] (cut eight 2" squares)
- Liquid adhesive[2]

For card
- 1 sheet white cardstock (cut one 2½" square; one 8½" x 5½" rectangle, fold in half)

- 1 sheet Berry Sponge paper[3] (cut one 2¾" square)
- Notched corner punch[4]
- Pink translucent ribbon ⅛" wide and 5" long
- Shrinky Dinks[5]
- Hand stamp[6]
- It's a girl stamp[7]
- Pink ink
- Ruler, scissors or paper cutter, hole punch

In this project: [1]Frances Meyer Inc.®, [2]Delta, [3]Making Memories, [4]Carl, [5]Klutz® or K& B Innovations Inc.®, [6]Stampa Rosa Inc.®, [7]All Night Media.

V-WING FOLD

Complete the following steps for each square:

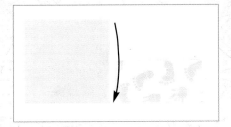

1. With the wrong side facing up, fold the top edge down to the bottom.

2. Fold the right edge down to the bottom edge, crease, and unfold.

3. Grasp the top right corner with your thumb inside the fold.

Push the upper right edge into the inside center of the fold and re-crease the diagonal edges.

4. Fold the lower right point of the top flap up to the top right corner, making a small triangle.

ASSEMBLY

1. Working with the first piece horizontally, place a small amount of adhesive on the left flap.

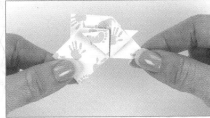

2. Working from the left, the next piece will sit with the bottom of the right point behind the triangle flap of the first piece. Snug the pieces up until the triangle points of each piece meet at the center bottom.

3. Continue adding pieces in this manner.

4. The first piece will sit inside the last to complete the pattern.

CARD ASSEMBLY

1. Stamp the hand on the Shrinky Dinks plastic. Cut around and punch a hole between the thumb and finger. Bake according to the manufacturers directions.

2. Corner punch the white square and the pink square.

3. Mount the white square centered on the pink square.

4. Mount the squares centered at the top of the folded white card.

5. Stamp the hand and greeting at the bottom of the card.

6. Tie a bow to the Shrinky Dinks hand, and glue the bow to the center of the folded element.

7. Mount the folded element centered on the white square.

8. Corner punch the white card.

Journal and Pen Set

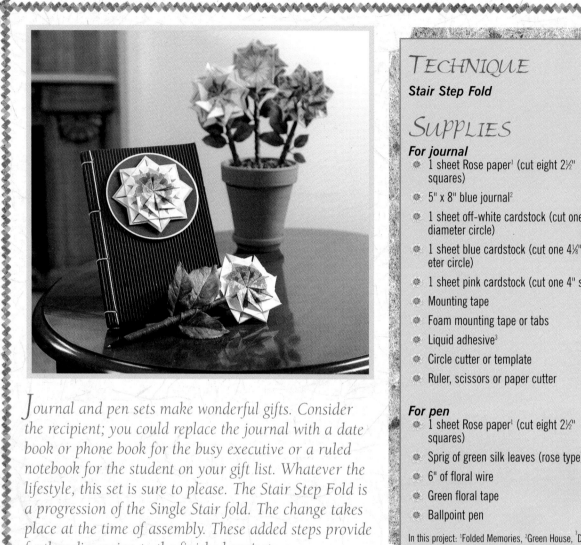

TECHNIQUE

Stair Step Fold

SUPPLIES

For journal

- 1 sheet Rose paper[1] (cut eight 2½" squares)
- 5" x 8" blue journal[2]
- 1 sheet off-white cardstock (cut one 4¼" diameter circle)
- 1 sheet blue cardstock (cut one 4⅛" diameter circle)
- 1 sheet pink cardstock (cut one 4" square)
- Mounting tape
- Foam mounting tape or tabs
- Liquid adhesive[3]
- Circle cutter or template
- Ruler, scissors or paper cutter

For pen

- 1 sheet Rose paper[1] (cut eight 2½" squares)
- Sprig of green silk leaves (rose type)
- 6" of floral wire
- Green floral tape
- Ballpoint pen

In this project: [1]Folded Memories, [2]Green House, [3]Delta.

Journal and pen sets make wonderful gifts. Consider the recipient; you could replace the journal with a date book or phone book for the busy executive or a ruled notebook for the student on your gift list. Whatever the lifestyle, this set is sure to please. The Stair Step Fold is a progression of the Single Stair fold. The change takes place at the time of assembly. These added steps provide further dimension to the finished project.

STAIR STEP FOLD

Complete steps #1–6 of the Triangle fold (page 18) for each square, followed by:

1 Position the triangle pieces so each shows this image.

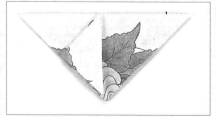

2 Fold the top left flap down to the center crease.

3 Bring the small folded flap (the stair) from the left over to the right.

ASSEMBLY

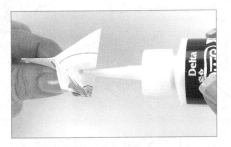

1 Place a small amount of adhesive between the two back flaps on the right side of the piece.

2 With the open edges at the top, place the single left flap of the next piece onto glue on the first piece. Snug the pieces together until they stop and the closed points meet.

3 Tuck the flap directly behind the stair into the top open edge of the piece behind it.

4 Continue in this manner with all eight pieces. Piece #1 will fit into piece #8 to complete the pattern. Don't forget to tuck in the flap on the last piece.

JOURNAL ASSEMBLY

1 Mount the folded element centered on the pink cardstock, and trim the excess to leave a ⅛" border.

2 Mount the pink cardstock centered on the blue circle with foam tape.

3 Mount the blue circle centered on the off-white circle.

4 Mount the off-white circle to the journal as desired with foam tape.

PEN ASSEMBLY

1 Follow the instructions for the Stair Step Fold on the previous page. Change the image at step #1 for a different finished look.

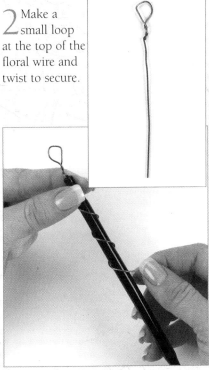

2 Make a small loop at the top of the floral wire and twist to secure.

3 Hold the loop above the flat end of the pen. Twist the wire around the pen, working in a downward spiral.

4 Starting at the top, use floral tape to wrap around the loop and pen, covering the wire. Leave only the tip of the pen exposed.

5 Line up a stem and leaves at about the halfway point of the length of the pen. Continue to wrap the pen with floral tape, covering and securing the stem.

6 Apply glue to the loop at the top of the pen. Slide the loop inside one of the open edges of the folded element.

Kitty

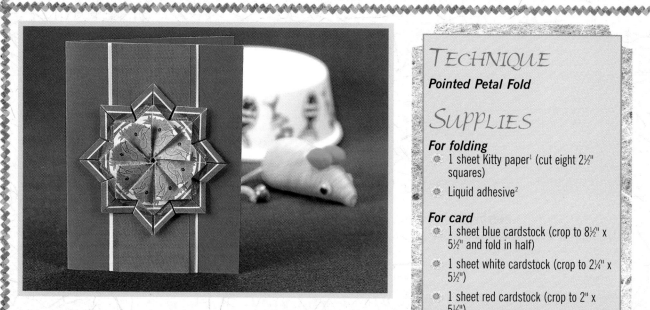

TECHNIQUE

Pointed Petal Fold

SUPPLIES

For folding
- 1 sheet Kitty paper[1] (cut eight 2½" squares)
- Liquid adhesive[2]

For card
- 1 sheet blue cardstock (crop to 8½" x 5½" and fold in half)
- 1 sheet white cardstock (crop to 2¼" x 5½")
- 1 sheet red cardstock (crop to 2" x 5½")
- 1 sheet purple cardstock (crop to 1¾" x 5½")
- Mounting tape
- Ruler, scissors or paper cutter

In this project: [1]Folded Memories paper provided in the middle of the book, [2]Delta.

*C*at got your tongue? Send a card instead! This one was made using the Pointed Petal Fold. The Pointed Petal has the greatest number of steps of any of the folds taught in this book. It may seem a daunting task but take heart. This fold is also one of the most versatile. Here you'll learn three different ways to assemble the Pointed Petal Fold, giving you many design options.

THE POINTED PETAL

Complete steps #1–6 of the Triangle Fold (page 18) for each piece, followed by:

1 Rotate the triangle pieces until the kitty's face shows in the middle of each.

2 Fold the top right flap over to the left side.

3 Fold the lower edge of the flap on the right side up to the center crease line.

4 Fold the top edge of the flap on the left down to the center crease line.

5 Slide your finger between the remaining long flaps on the left.

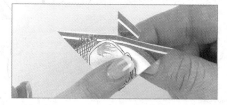

Push the top flaps over to the right side.

6 Fold the lower edge of the flap on the left side up to the center crease line.

7 Fold the top edge of the flap on the right down to the center crease line.

8 Fold the top right flap over to the left.

ASSEMBLY #1

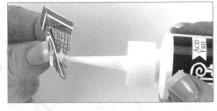

1 With your left hand, pick up the first piece. Apply a small amount of adhesive to the back right flap.

2 With your right hand, place the left side of the second piece in between the two right flaps of the first piece. Push it in until the pieces are snug against each other and the bottom points meet.

3 Continue adding pieces in this fashion.

4 The first piece will slide into the last to complete the pattern.

CARD ASSEMBLY

1 Layer the purple strip on the red strip and the red strip on the white strip, centering each and securing with mounting tape.

2 Center the colored strips on the blue card, and secure with mounting tape.

3 Center the folded element on the card, and secure with mounting tape.

FOLDED ASSEMBLY #2

For this assembly, you'll need eight of the triangle pieces. Four pieces should show a different part of the image of the original paper. The remaining four pieces should all show the same image.

1 Cut a small scrap of paper about 1½" square.

2 Position the four folded pieces on top of the scrap with the different images so that the diamonds form a square, and recreate the center of the picture of the Kitty paper. Secure from behind with adhesive.

3 Slide a new folded piece in the space between two of the previously secured pieces. Line up the outer points of the diamond of the back piece with the edge of the center square. Secure with adhesive from behind.

4 Add the three remaining pieces in the same manner.

5 If necessary, trim the scrap paper so that it doesn't show from the front.

FOLDED ASSEMBLY #3

This fold can also be assembled as a border.
Work with the pieces horizontally and with the diamonds pointing to the right.

1 Lift up the diamond flaps of the left piece pinching them together, and slide the point of the left piece into the space between the two petals of the right piece.

2 Secure with adhesive.

3 Replace the pinched diamond flaps to their original position, and continue adding the remaining pieces in this manner.

Joy

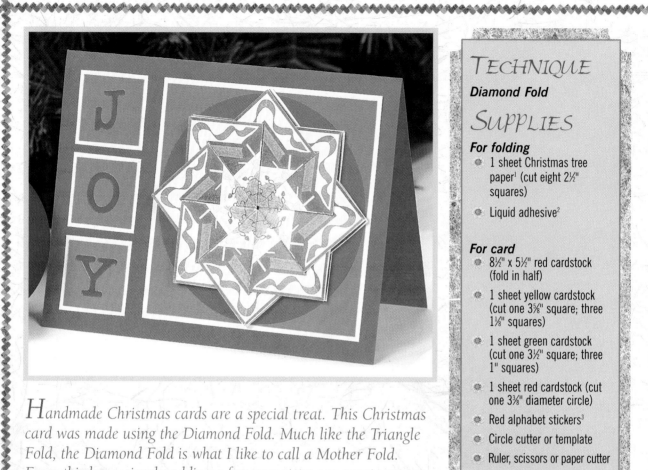

TECHNIQUE
Diamond Fold

SUPPLIES
For folding
- 1 sheet Christmas tree paper[1] (cut eight 2½" squares)
- Liquid adhesive[2]

For card
- 8½" x 5½" red cardstock (fold in half)
- 1 sheet yellow cardstock (cut one 3⅜" square; three 1⅛" squares)
- 1 sheet green cardstock (cut one 3½" square; three 1" squares)
- 1 sheet red cardstock (cut one 3⅜" diameter circle)
- Red alphabet stickers[3]
- Circle cutter or template
- Ruler, scissors or paper cutter

In this project: [1]Folded Memories paper provided in the middle of the book, [2]Delta, [3]Frances Meyer.

*H*andmade Christmas cards are a special treat. This Christmas card was made using the Diamond Fold. Much like the Triangle Fold, the Diamond Fold is what I like to call a Mother Fold. From this base, simply adding a few new steps can create many different finished shapes and effects. Once you're familiar with the Diamond Fold, you'll easily master many other folds found in this book.

DIAMOND FOLD
Complete the following steps for each square:

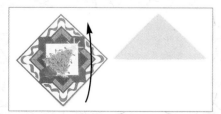

1 Position the first square as a diamond with the right side up. Fold the bottom point up to form a triangle.

2 Open the piece flat. Fold the left point over to right.

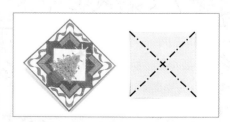

3 Open the piece flat. Flip the piece over so the wrong side is facing up.

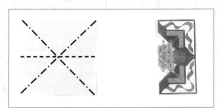

4 Fold the piece in half to make a rectangle.

5 Open the piece flat, and repeat step #4, folding side to side.

6 With both hands, grasp the folded edge of the piece. Bring both thumbs toward the center, forming a layered diamond shape. There will be two flaps on each side.

7 Choosing your pattern: To create the repetitive pattern shown in this project, rotate the flaps of your finished pieces until all eight pieces show the star on the right side.

ASSEMBLY

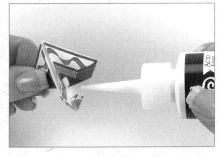

1 Pick up piece #1 with the closed point at the bottom. Slightly open the flaps on the right side, and place a small amount of adhesive in the crease.

2 With your other hand, pick up piece #2. Place the top left flap of piece #2 between the two flaps of the right side of piece #1, so the star shows on top. Slide the pieces together until they stop and the bottom points meet.

3 Repeat steps #1 and #2 with all eight pieces. After piece #8, bring the flaps of piece #1 forward and into

piece #8 to properly continue the pattern. There may be a small hole in the center. Add additional adhesive as necessary.

CARD ASSEMBLY

1 Mount each of the 1" green squares centered on the 1⅛" yellow squares.

2 Center the letters J, O, and Y, one on each square.

3 Mount the red circle to the 3½" green square

4 Mount the green square to the 3⅝" yellow square.

5 Mount the folded element centered on the red circle

6 Place the red cardstock so that the fold is at the top, and mount the 3⅝" yellow square centered ¼" from the right side.

7 Mount the J square centered ¼" from the upper left side.

8 Mount the Y square centered ¼" from the lower left side.

9 Mount the O square centered between the J and Y squares.

This is what the repetive pattern looks like from the back.

Make Your Own Envelopes

*H*andmade cards can be unusual sizes or slightly more bulky than store-bought cards, making it troublesome to find an envelope. Now you'll never be at a loss for envelopes, because you can make your own! Working with common household materials like gift-wrap, magazine pages, or computer paper, follow this formula to make envelopes for any size or shape of card.

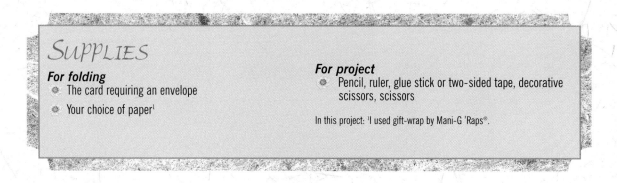

Supplies

For folding
- The card requiring an envelope
- Your choice of paper¹

For project
- Pencil, ruler, glue stick or two-sided tape, decorative scissors, scissors

In this project: ¹I used gift-wrap by Mani-G 'Raps®.

Folding Your Envelope

1 Place the card centered on the paper. Fold the right and left edges in over the card.

2 Fold the bottom edge up over the card. Make a small mark on each side along the top edge of the flap.

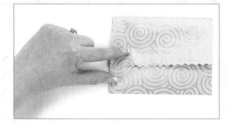

3 Fold the top edge down over the card, and crease well.

4 Unfold the top and bottom flaps and remove the card.

5 Use the scissors to cut diagonally from the marked point on each side out to the crease line. Continue cutting, following the crease, to remove the upper portion of the right and left flaps.

6 From the marked point down, apply glue to the top sections of the right and left flaps.

7 Fold the bottom flap up, and apply pressure to seal the outside edges.

8 Replace the card. Fold the top flap down and trim with decorative scissors if desired.

9 Seal the edge with glue or a sticker. Now you can address, stamp, and mail your creation.

Formulas

Formula for measuring:
Card length + 1½"
Card width doubled + 1½"

For example:
If your card is 5½" x 4¼" you'll need paper cut to:
Length 5½" + 1½" = 7"
Width 4¼" + 4¼" + 1½" = 10"
= 7" x 10"

Using a square card of 4" x 4", you'll need paper cut to:
Length 4" + 1½" = 5½"
Width 4" + 4" + 1½" = 9½"
= 5½" x 9½"

Chapter 3 Scrapbooking

11. Soccer
page 34

12. Hayli
page 36

13. Picking Strawberries
page 38

14. Wedding
page 40

15. Award Ribbon
page 42

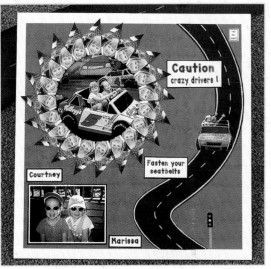

16. Crazy Driver
page 44

17. America
page 46

18. Harvest
page 48

19. Hawaii
page 50

20. Snowmen
page 52

Soccer

Garrett Mason #5
Fireballs
Terrace-Brier Soccer club 2000

Calling all soccer Moms! Here is a page just for you. Creating interesting sports pages has just become easier. Use this folded ball to add dimension to your next soccer page. Not a soccer fan? No problem. Change the paper color, and you can create a folded baseball or basketball using the same techniques.

TECHNIQUE

Pointed Petal Fold

SUPPLIES

For folding
- 2 sheets black-with-speckle paper[1] (cut ten 3" squares)
- 3¾" diameter circle template
- Liquid adhesive[2]

For page
- 2 sheets 12" x 12" blue paper
- 1 sheet 12" x 12" green paper
- 1 sheet 12" x 12" white paper
- 1 sheet 8½" x 11" black paper
- 1 sheet 8½" x 11" red paper
- White marker[3]
- Black marker
- Blue chalk
- Mounting tape, scissors or paper cutter

In this project: [1]Provo Craft, [2]Delta, [3]Milky Way from Galaxy Markers.

POINTED PETAL FOLD

With five squares print side up and five squares wrong side up, follow the instructions for the Pointed Petal Fold (page 26). You'll end up with five black folded pieces and five white folded pieces.

ASSEMBLY

1 Working with the pieces horizontally, place a small amount of adhesive on the back of the diamond point of one piece.

2 Alternating colors, insert the point into the space in the end of the lower leg of the next piece.

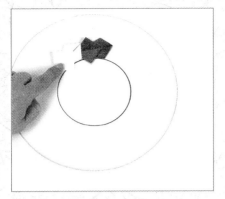

3 Lay the pieces on a 3¾" diameter circle template. Adjust the pieces so that the lower leg of each piece lines up with the outer edge of the circle template. The diamond points will extend into the circle.

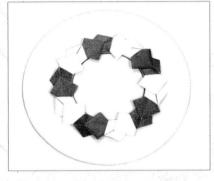

4 Continue this process with all 10 pieces. The first piece will fit into the last to complete the circle.

PAGE ASSEMBLY

1 Use a die cut or freehand cut the grass from the green paper. Mount grass to the bottom of the blue pages.

2 Use a die cut, or freehand cut the cleat from the black paper. Embellish it with a white pen.

3 Mount the cleat partly off the left side of one of the blue pages, pointing up toward the opposite corner. Trim the excess from the overhang. Add laces on the blue background with black pen.

4 Mount your photo in the folded ball.

5 Mount the folded ball to the upper left corner of the other blue page.

USE THE SOCCER BALL ASSEMBLY ON A GREETING CARD

(Folded Memories Kitty paper is provided in the middle of the book.)

1 Choose any repetitive pattern you wish for this assembly.

2 Refer to the assembly instructions for the Soccer Ball above. To adapt the assembly for an eight piece element: On step #3, disregard the circle template and be sure that the inserted piece is sitting squarely in the opening of the previous piece.

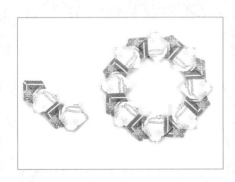

12

Hayli

The left side kite fold and the Flower Trio paper add an elegant accent to any photo. In this example, the Flower Trio paper and green leaves compliment the garden in the background of the photos and the flower on Hayli's hat. Choose photos that will go with these papers, or substitute colors or patterns to accent any special moment.

TECHNIQUE

Left Side Kite Fold

SUPPLIES

For folding
- 2 sheets Flower Trio paper[1] (cut fifteen 2½" squares)
- 2¾" circle template
- Liquid adhesive[2]

For page
- 2 sheets 12" x 12" white paper
- 1 sheet 12" x 12" fuchsia paper[3] (cut one 11¾" square)
- 1 sheet green paper
- White marker[4]
- Circle cutter or circle template
- Fine point green pen
- Notched corner punch[5]
- Mounting tape, ruler, scissors or paper cutter

In this project: [1]Folded Memories paper provided in the middle of the book, [2]Delta, [3]Scrapbook Adventures®, [4]Milky Way from Galaxy Markers, [5]Carl.

LEFT SIDE KITE FOLD

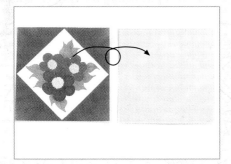

Turn all squares so that the image looks like this. Flip the stack over to the right so the wrong side is facing up. Complete the following steps for each square:

1 Fold the bottom edge up to the top.

2 Fold the bottom left corner up to the top edge.

3 Lift the flap up, and press the crease straight down to create a kite shape.

ASSEMBLY

1 Working around a 2¾" circle template, place the lower left edge of the kite of the first piece anywhere on the outside of the circle template. Place a small amount of adhesive on the lower right side of the piece.

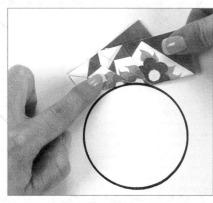

2 Place the left point of the kite of the next piece behind the kite of the first piece. The top point of the kite on piece #2 will line up with the top edge of the piece beneath it. The left edge of the kite will line up with the circle template.

3 Continue adding pieces in this manner around the template.

4 The first piece will lie on top of the last to complete the pattern

PAGE ASSEMBLY

1 Punch all four corners of the fuchsia paper with the notched corner punch.

2 Center the fuchsia paper on white paper, and tape it down.

3 Using the green paper, cut a 6¼" circle with a 5¾" circle cut out of the center.

4 Using the green paper, freehand cut five leaves of varying sizes from 2" to 4" long, and cut two squiggles 3" to 4" long.

5 Mount your photo in the folded element, and mount the element to the other sheet of white paper. Cut a ⅛" border around the folded element.

6 Position the green circle in the upper left corner of the fuchsia paper.

7 Mount the folded element to the center of the green circle.

8 Arrange the leaves and squiggles, as desired, along the top and side of the folded element. Tape or glue them in place.

9 Matt additional photos with the remaining white paper, and arrange them as desired on the page.

10 With the white marker, creatively write the name of the person or persons in the photos. If you're not comfortable with your own writing, many alphabet templates are available.

13

Picking Strawberries

Create a great border or sidebar with this fun folded fruit. A few simple adjustments to the Diamond fold and voilà! You've got strawberries.

TECHNIQUE

Strawberry Fold

SUPPLIES

For folding
- 1 sheet 8½" x 11" red-with-white-dot paper1 (cut three 3" squares; one 1¾" square)
- Liquid adhesive[2]

For page
- 1 sheet 12" x 12" dark red paper
- 1 sheet 12" x 12" green paper (cut one 3¼" x 11¼" rectangle; one 3⅛" x 3¾" rectangle; save the remainder)

- 1 sheet 8½" x 11" red-with-white-dot paper[1] (cut one 2¾" x 11" rectangle; one 3" x 3⅝" rectangle)
- 1 sheet 8½" x 11" white-with-red-dot paper[1] (crop to 2½" x 10⅝"; save the remainder)
- 1 sheet white paper
- Daisy punch[3]
- Green fine point pen
- Scalloped scissors[4]
- Mounting tape
- Ruler, scissors or paper cutter

In this project: [1]The Paper Patch®, [2]Delta, [3]Family Treasures®, [4]Fiskars®.

STRAWBERRY FOLD

Begin by following steps #1–6 of the Diamond Fold (page 28) with all four of the red-with-white-dot squares, followed by:

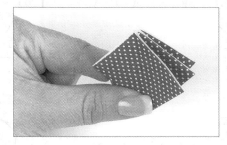

1 Fold the top left flap over to the right. There will be three flaps on the right and one on the left.

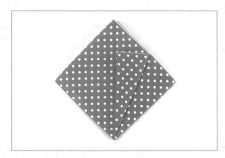

2 Fold the lower right side of the flap on the right into the center crease.

3 Slide your finger between the two back flaps on the right; push the top flaps over to the left side.

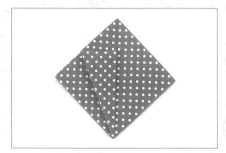

4 Repeat step #2 on the left side.

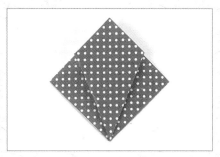

5 Return the top folded flap from the left to the right.

6 Pick up the piece. While lightly pinching the bottom of the folded edges, fold the open point to the back. Secure with adhesive.

7 Fold the left and right side points to the back to soften the outer edges.

8 Fold a green daisy punch over the top to complete the strawberry look. Secure with adhesive.

PAGE ASSEMBLY

1 Make the sidebar:

 a. Mount the large red-with-white-dot rectangle centered on the large green rectangle.

 b. Mount the large white-with-red-dot rectangle centered on the large red-with-white-dot rectangle.

 c. Create the vine by cutting a slightly wavy strip 10⅜" long and about ¼" wide out of the remaining green paper

 d. Create five large leaves and one small leaf by cutting heart shapes with the scalloped scissors. Embellish the leaves with a green fine point pen.

 e. Mount the vine, three large strawberries, and five large leaves on the white-with-red-dot rectangle, as desired.

 f. Mount the sidebar to the red paper, centered ¼" from the right side

2 Mount the 3" x 3⅝" red-with-white-dot rectangle centered on the 3⅛" x 3¾" green rectangle.

3 Journal on the white paper and trim as needed to fit inside the journal matting.

4 Mount the small strawberry and small leaf at the bottom of your journaling.

5 Matt and mount the remaining papers according to the size of your photos.

6 Mount journaling and photos to the page as desired.

14

Wedding

Kari, Krista, and Lila on
Chris and Krista's
Wedding day
February 19, 2000

*M*any folds create circular openings. The Lapel Fold is one of the few that can be assembled as a rectangle or a square. Its angular shape can create interesting geometric patterns inside the opening. In this example, the use of vellum adds further dimension because it allows you to see areas of the fold that would not show with opaque paper.

TECHNIQUE
Lapel Fold

SUPPLIES
For folding
- 1 sheet 12" x 12" vellum[1] (cut ten 2" squares)
- Adhesive[2]

For page
- 1 sheet 12" x 12" vellum[1]
- 2 sheets 12" x 12" two-sided lavender/eggshell paper[3]
- Ruler, scissors or paper cutter

In this project: [1]It Takes Two®, [2]Glue Dots®; [3]Anna Griffin Inc.

LAPEL FOLD

Complete the following steps for each square:

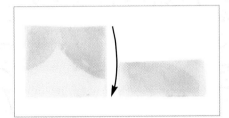

1 With the wrong side of the square facing up, fold the top edge down to the bottom.

2 Fold the left edge of the top flap up to the top edge.

3 Fold the right edge of the top flap up to the top edge.

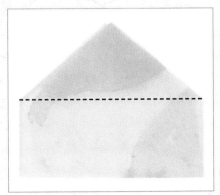

4 Lift the top flap.

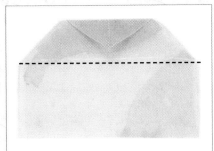

5 Fold the top point down to the center crease.

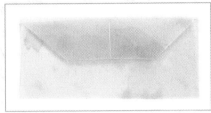

6 Fold the top flap down along the center crease line.

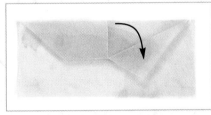

7 Fold the top right edge down to the right creating a long triangle.

8 Repeat step #7 on the left side.

ASSEMBLY

1 Use eight pieces to make four corners. For each corner, hold one piece vertically with the folded edge to the left; hold the next piece horizontally with the folded edge to the top. Place the left edge of the horizontal piece in the space between the fold and flat back of the vertical piece, creating a right angle. Secure with a Glue Dot between the back flaps.

2 Prepare a 3½" x 5¾" rectangle of the lavender/eggshell paper. (If you're using computer-generated journaling, print it on the eggshell side before cropping the paper.) Adhere the folded corners to the paper with the eggshell side up. The folded pieces will slightly overlap.

3 Center the two remaining folded pieces in each space between the corner pieces, and secure with adhesive.

PROJECT ASSEMBLY

1 Crop and mount photos on the lavender paper as desired.

2 Arrange the photos and folded element on the vellum square, and tape them down.

3 Use Glue Dots to mount the vellum to your scrapbook page. If you're using slide-in pages, mount the vellum square to a sheet of white paper before putting it into the scrapbook sleeve.

15

Award Ribbon

The
1999
International
Fjord Horse Show
held in
Libby, Montana
~
Sheri on Huldra
and
Julie on Gustaf
won
1st place

*K*now anyone who's won an award lately? This fold makes a great mock award ribbon. It can be used for any occasion, from the classroom to the sports field to international competition. Change the colors accordingly and it will be a great accent for documenting your event. You don't have to use it in a scrapbook though; you may want to frame your page and hang it where others can see it and appreciate the accomplishment.

TECHNIQUE

Upright Kite Fold

SUPPLIES

For folding

- 1 sheet blue paper (cut eight 2½" squares)
- Liquid adhesive[1]

For page

- 2 sheets 12" x 12" black paper

- 1 sheet 12 " x 12" striped paper[2] (crop to 11½" x 11½")
- 1 sheet blue paper (cut 2 strips of 1¼" x 3" each; save the remainder)
- 1 sheet white paper (cut 2 strips of 1" x 3" each; one 2" diameter circle)
- Decorative scissors
- Gold number stickers
- Mounting tape
- Ruler, scissors or paper cutter

In this project: [1]Delta, [2]Frances Meyer.

Upright Kite Fold

Complete the following steps for each square:

1 Follow step #1 of the Triangle Fold (page 18), but keep the wrong side of the paper facing up. Follow steps #2–4 of the Triangle Fold, but don't flip the piece over at step #3.

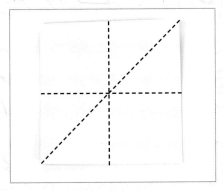

2 Open the piece flat. The wrong side should be facing up.

3 Fold the lower left corner over to the upper right (don't crease).

4 Push the lower right corner up to the top right corner, making a square. Crease all edges.

5 Lift the upper left point straight up.

6 Press straight down on the crease, squishing the flap flat into a kite shape.

Assembly

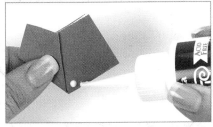

1 On piece #1, place a small amount of adhesive on the right flap near the lower point of the kite.

2 Place the left kite edge of piece #2 against the right kite edge of piece #1. The top right point of piece #2 should be just above the bottom edge of piece #1.

3 Continue adding pieces in this manner.

4 The first piece will slide inside the last to complete the element.

Project Assembly

1 Mount the striped paper centered on the black paper.

2 Mount the white strips centered on the blue strips.

3 Mount the blue strips extending out from the bottom of the folded element.

4 Cut around the 2" white circle with the decorative scissors, and place a "1" sticker in the middle of the white circle.

5 Mount the white circle in the center of the folded element. (It should resemble an award ribbon.)

6 Prepare the photo and journaling.

7 Matt the photo and journaling with the remaining paper, and apply them to the scrapbook page as desired.

8 Mount the folded element to the page.

16

Crazy Driver

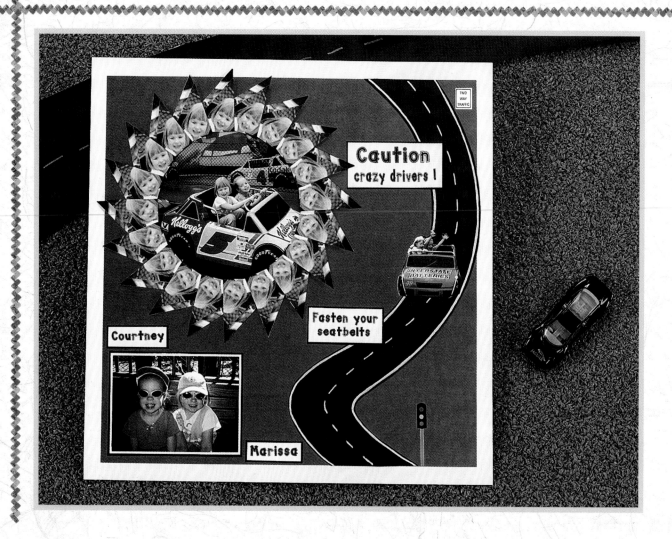

Ask any kindergartener, "What's one of the first things you learned about in school?" and they will likely tell you about patterns. Patterns are all around us, in math, in art, in life. Patterns are fun! You can make a pattern out of any-thing, which is why I love this project. In this example, scanning the focal photo into my home computer gave me the ability to generate my own patterned folding paper. This paper just so happens to feature my kindergartener. If you don't have a home computer, use a color copier to create your own pattern paper.

TECHNIQUE

Two-Step Frame Fold

SUPPLIES

For folding

- Scanner or digital camera
- Personal computer
- Printer paper
- 4¼" circle template
- Liquid adhesive[1]

For page

- 1 sheet 12" x 12" yellow paper
- 1 sheet 8½" x 11" yellow paper
- 1 sheet 12" x 12" red paper (crop to 11" square)
- 1 sheet 12" x 12" black paper
- Computer journaling CD[2]
- Yellow opaque marker
- Road sign stickers
- Mounting tape
- Ruler, scissors or paper cutter

In this project: [1]Delta, [2]Page Printables® from Cock-a-Doodle Designs.

PREPARING THE PAPER

1 Scan or import a photo into your computer.

2 Choose the image in the photo that you want to be the focus of the repetitive pattern. Crop the photo into a 2 1/2" square, so that the desired image is to the left and just above the center of the square.

3 Print and cut 21 squares.

TWO STEP FRAME FOLD

Complete the following steps for each square:

1 Hold the square so that the pattern side is facing you. Fold the lower left corner back and up to the upper right corner to make a triangle.

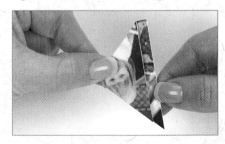

2 Fold the upper left point down and over to the right. Stop approximately ¼" from the right edge so that the two edges are parallel.

ASSEMBLY

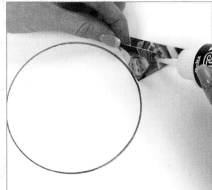

1 Working around a 4¼" circle template, place the lower left folded edge of the first piece anywhere along the template. Apply a small amount of adhesive between the flaps.

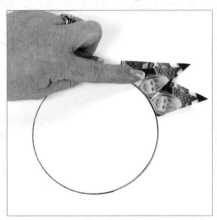

2 Place the left side of the next piece about ⅜" in between the flaps of the first. Line up the extended edge with the template.

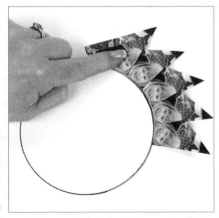

3 Continue adding pieces in this manner.

4 The first piece will sit inside the last to complete the pattern.

PAGE ASSEMBLY

1 Mount the red square centered on the yellow square.

2 Secure the photo inside the folded frame, and mount the frame to the upper left side of the red square. Let the points slightly extend on the yellow paper at the top and side.

3 Crop the black paper to resemble a road, approximately 1½" wide and 12" long. Embellish the road with a yellow marker, and mount it to the right side of the page.

4 Print journaling on yellow paper, and matt it with the remaining black paper.

5 Matt and arrange additional photos on the page.

6 Add stickers to compliment the page theme.

America

There's nothing quite like capturing the patriotic spirit in America's children. The events of 2001, in New York and around the world, have reminded Americans of the importance of patriotism and the privilege of freedom. This scrapbook page uses a combination of two different folds to create a frame for this photo of brothers Geoffrey and Scott Gilham, who are proud to be Americans!

TECHNIQUE

Pointed Petal Corner Fold

SUPPLIES

For folding
- 3 sheets 12" x 12" Patriotic Tea-Bag Stars paper[1] (Cut along lines to get 2" squares. This paper contains two patterns. Use the one-directional stripe ones only. A total of 35 squares are needed.)

- Liquid adhesive[2]

For page
- 1 sheet 12" x 12" Small Stars on Blue paper[1]
- 1 sheet 12" x 12" white paper (crop to 10⅜" x 11")
- 2 sheets 12" x 12" red paper (cut one 10½" x 10¾" rectangle; one 7⅞" x 5⅞" rectangle)
- America Overalls™ die cuts[3]
- Ruler, scissors or paper cutter

In this project: [1]Design Originals, [2]Delta, [3]EK Success.

THE POINTED PETAL CORNER

Before you begin, set aside seven squares to use later. With the remaining 28 squares, follow steps #1–6 of the Triangle Fold (page 18), followed by:

1 Rotate flaps until all pieces show the vertical stripe

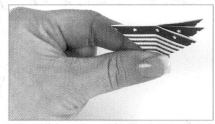

2 Fold the top left flap over to the right. There will be three flaps on the right and one on the left.

3 Fold the top edge of the right flap down to the center crease line.

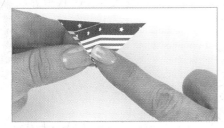

4 Slide a finger between the two full flaps on the right, and push the top flaps over to the left.

5 Fold the top edge of the left flap down to the center crease line.

6 Push the top folded flap back over to the right.

TRANSITION PIECES

Fold the remaining seven squares as follows:

1 Fold the square in half so that the right side faces out and the stripes are horizontal.

2 Open the piece flat, and position it as a diamond. Fold the corners into the center.

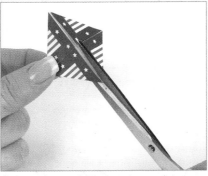

3 Cut the folded piece in half along the center crease.

FRAME ASSEMBLY

Part one:

1 Using the smaller red rectangle as a guide, start at the top left corner. Line up the point of the diamond shape of one piece with the edge of the guide. Allow the long flap to fall behind the guide. Secure with adhesive from behind.

2 Place the next piece so that the long edge meets that of the first piece, forming a point. Secure with adhesive from behind.

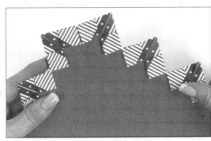

3 Continue adding pieces in this manner to cover all sides.

Part two:

1 To add the transitional pieces, place a small amount of adhesive on the lower edge of one of the remaining triangle pieces.

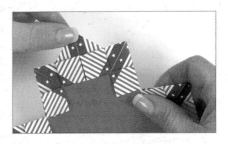

2 Slide the piece behind the corner of the frame until the bottom blue line is covered. Repeat for all corners.

3 Use the remaining pieces, in the same manner, to fill in the spaces between the previously mounted pieces of part one.

PAGE ASSEMBLY

1 Mount your photo centered on the folded frame.

2 Mount the folded frame to the large red rectangle centered 1/4" from the top.

3 Cut out the America, heart, and star. Mount them in the open space below the folded frame, as desired.

4 Mount the large red rectangle centered on the white rectangle.

5 Mount the white rectangle centered on the star paper.

Harvest

TECHNIQUE

Checkmark Fold

SUPPLIES

For folding
- 2 sheets Scarecrow folding paper[1] (cut twenty-two 2½" squares)
- Liquid adhesive[2]

For page
- 4 sheets 8½" x 11" black paper (cut two 5¾" diameter circles; save the remainder)
- 2 sheets green paper (cut two 5" diameter circles; save the remainder)
- 2 sheets orange plaid paper[3] (crop each to 8 ¼" x 11¾")
- 2 sheets orange paper (cut two 5¼" diameter circles)
- Computer journaling CD[4]
- Black fine point marker
- Circle cutter or template
- Mounting tape, ruler, scissors or paper cutter

In this project: [1]Folded Memories paper provided in the middle of the book, [2]Delta, [3]Daisy Ds, [4]Creative Lettering Volume 3 by Creating Keepsakes.

*W*hen I look at my photo stash (OK, truth, giant heaping basket), I am always amazed at how many pictures we take at harvest time. Pumpkin farms, corn mazes, and trick-or-treat just to name a few. Many requests for harvest paper have come my way so I must not be the only one with an abundance of fall photos. Here are a few photos from my harvest stash, featuring the Scarecrow folding paper included in this book.

CHECKMARK FOLD

Before you begin, lay all of the folding squares so that the Scarecrow is on his side with his head to the right. Flip the stack over to the right so the wrong side is facing up. Complete the following steps for each square:

1 Fold the bottom edge up toward the top. Stop 3/16" from the top edge.

2 Fold the bottom left corner up to the top edge.

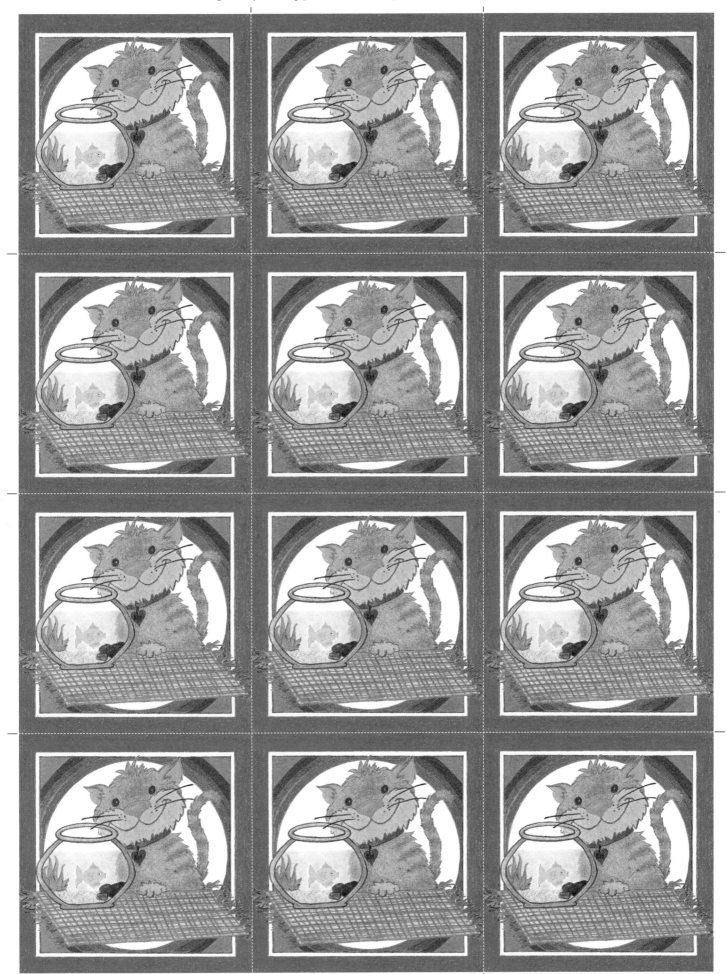

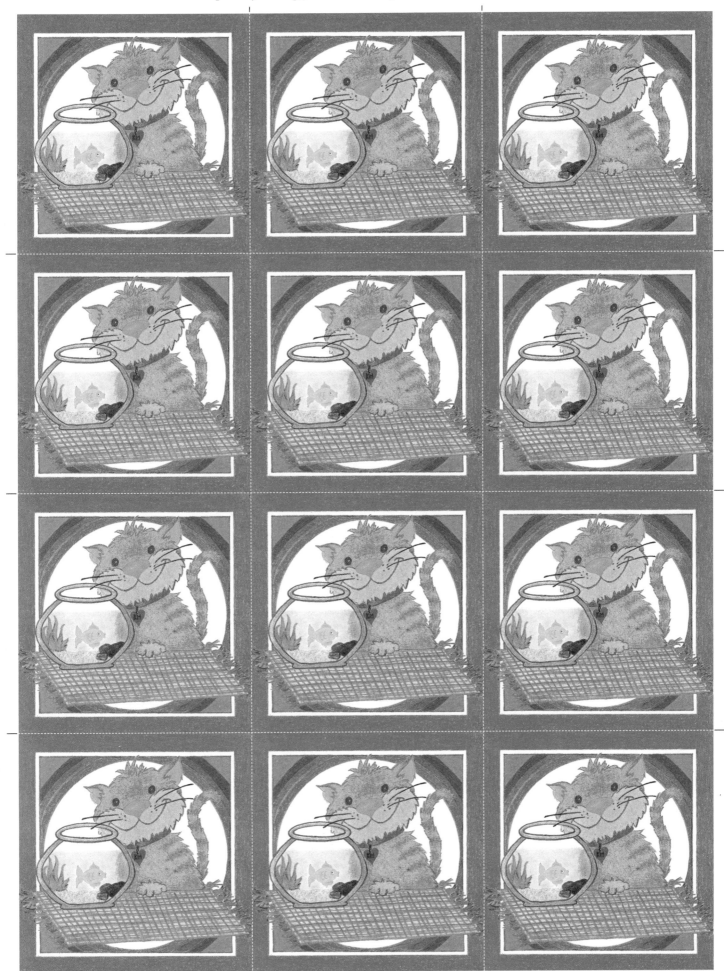

3 Flip the piece over so that the short folded edge is at the top and the sharp point is on the left.

4 Lift the lower right corner (top layer only) up toward the top, so that the bottom edge meets the left side and forms a long triangle.

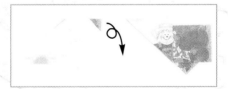

5 Flip the piece over so the scarecrow is on the top.

ASSEMBLY

Use 11 pieces for each folded element.

1 Working with the first piece, so that the point is at the left, place a small amount of adhesive on the lower right side of the piece.

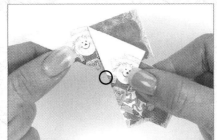

2 Hold the second piece so that the point is up. Lay the second piece on top of the first. Line up the left folded edge of piece #2 with the right folded edge of piece #1. Allow the folded edge of piece #2 to extend about ¾" below piece #1. The right shoulder of the Scarecrow should meet the bottom of the first piece.

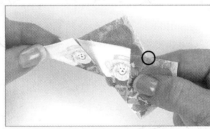

Slightly angle piece #2 so that the point falls just behind the flap of piece #1 and the top right edge of piece #2 covers the bottom corner of piece #1.

3 Add the remaining pieces in the same manner.

4 The first piece will lie on top of the last to complete the pattern.

PAGE ASSEMBLY

1 Center the orange plaid paper on the black paper, and secure with mounting tape.

2 Layer the circles in this order: green on top of orange, and orange on top of black. Center eachone and secure between layers with mounting tape. Make two sets of circles.

3 Mount your photos into the folded elements.

4 Center the folded elements, one on each circle set, and secure with mounting tape.

5 Crop and mat your photos with the remaining green and black papers, as desired.

6 Lay the two plaid background pieces side by side. Mount one of the folded elements to the lower left side of the page on the left.

7 Mount the remaining folded element to the upper right side of the page on the right.

8 Prepare the page title.

9 Mount the page title and remaining photos to the pages as desired.

19

Hawaii

One of the fundamental principals of creating a good scrapbook page is to draw out components or colors from the photos. In this example, the flower leis in the photo are so beautiful it seemed a natural choice to recreate the feel with a folded lei on the page.

TECHNIQUE

Two Step Variation Fold

SUPPLIES

For folding

- 2 sheets 12" x 12" floral paper[1] (cut thirty-six 2" squares)
- Liquid adhesive[2]

For page

- 2 sheets 12" x 12" lemon yellow paper[3]

- 1 sheet 12" x 12" pink slush paper[4]
- 1 sheet mint green paper
- 1 sheet white paper
- 1 sheet tan paper
- 1 large palm tree die cut
- 2 feet yellow wraphia[5]
- Pink, green, and black marking pens
- Mounting tape
- Ruler, scissors or paper cutter

In this project: [1]MM Colors by Design, [2]Delta, [3]Making Memories, [4]Carolee's Creations, [5]Berwick®.

Two Step Variation Fold

Complete the following steps for each square:

1 Complete the first two steps of the Two Step Frame Fold on page 44.

2 Lift the top flap straight up.

3 Press straight down on the crease, squishing the flap into a flat diamond shape.

Assembly

Use eight pieces for each folded element; you'll make four and a half total.

1 Pick up piece #1 with the closed point at the bottom. Slightly lift the diamond flap on the right side, and place a small amount of adhesive in the crease.

2 With your other hand, pick up piece #2. Place the left side of the diamond shape of piece #2 behind the diamond flap on the right side of piece #1. Slide the pieces together until they stop and the bottom points meet.

3 Continue adding pieces in this manner.

4 After adding piece #8, bring the diamond of piece #1 forward and into piece #8 to properly continue the pattern. There may be a small hole in the center. Add additional adhesive as necessary.

Page Assembly

1 Measure and cut a white rectangle twice as wide as the photo you're featuring. Mount the photo to the left side.

2 Mount the white rectangle (postcard) to the mint green paper. Trim the excess, leaving a ⅛" matting.

3 Mount the green rectangle on the lemon yellow paper. Trim the excess, leaving a ⅛" matting.

4 Mount the yellow rectangle to the pink paper. Trim the excess, leaving a ⅛" matting.

5 Journal on the white rectangle to resemble a postcard.

6 Mount the palm tree die cut on the left edge of the 12" lemon yellow square.

7 Position the postcard at an angle, allowing the bottom corner to extend off the page, and tape it down.

8 Freehand cut the tan paper to resemble sand, and tape it to the bottom edge of the page.

9 Run the wraphia through the small holes in the four folded elements.

10 Tape the half element with the wraphia under it to the left edge of the page.

11 Position the remaining folded elements around the bottom edge of the page, and tape them down to resemble a lei.

12 Write the greeting at the top of the page.

13 Trim the excess paper that extends beyond the page.

20

Snowmen

*S*pecialty folding papers can be used in a number of ways. Here I have used them not only folded but also as die cut letters and a character embellishment. This is a great way to use up extra squares and compliment the folded element on your page.

TECHNIQUE

Half Fold-Back

SUPPLIES

For folding
- 2 sheets Snowmen paper[1] (cut 17 squares)
- Liquid adhesive[2]

For page
- 5 squares of Snowmen paper[1] (4 squares for die cutting, 1 for embellishment)

- 2 sheets 12" x 12" white paper
- 2 sheets 12" x 12" red paper (cut one 10⅞" square; save the remainder)
- 1 sheet 12" x 12" blue spotted paper[3] (cut one 10½" square)
- 3 snowflake die cuts[4]
- Foam mounting dots[5]
- Mounting tape
- Ruler, scissors or paper cutter

In this project: [1]Folded Memories, [2]Delta, [3]Making Memories, [4]Accu-Cut®, [5]All Night Media.

Note: Die cut machines are available for use in many scrapbook stores. If you do not access to a die cut machine, trace letters using an alphabet template.

THE HALF FOLD-BACK

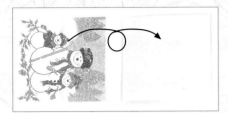

Before you begin, turn the 17 folding squares on their side so that the snowman with the blue scarf is at the bottom and the snowmen heads are at the right. Flip the stack over to the right. Now the heads are at the left and the wrong side of the paper is facing up. Complete the following steps for each square:

1 Fold the bottom edge up to the top. You should see the blue snowman again (heads are at the left).

2 Fold the bottom left corner up to the center of the top edge.

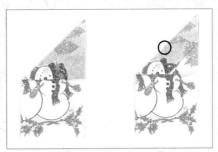

3 Turn the piece so that the point is at the top. Take the tip of the small triangle that was created by step #2 and fold it up and over to the middle of the folded edge.

ASSEMBLY

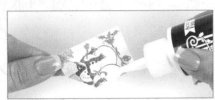

1 Working with the folded pieces horizontally and from the right, place a small amount of liquid adhesive on the bottom blue mitten on the first piece.

2 Slide the point of piece #2 behind the flap of the first piece piece. Stop when the point of the small triangle meets the bottom edge of the flap.

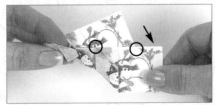

Keeping the small triangle point snug with the bottom edge, rotate the piece down until the top point almost shows from behind the flap of the other piece. You can also use the printed image as a point of reference. For example, look at the upper edge where one piece lays atop the other. It should line up near the snowman's buttons at the left and the holly leaves at the right.

3 Continue in this manner with all pieces. The last piece slides behind the first to complete the pattern.

PAGE ASSEMBLY

1 Mount the red 10⅞" square centered on the 12" x 12" white background.

2 Mount the blue 10½" square centered on the red square.

3 Place your photo behind the folded frame and secure with adhesive.

4 Mount the folded frame to the remaining red paper. Trim the excess, leaving a ⅛" matting around the frame.

5 Mount the matted frame to the remaining white paper. Trim the excess, leaving a 1/16" matting around the frame.

6 Mount the folded frame to the blue square toward the upper right corner.

7 Die cut the letters S, N, O, W out of four of the snowman squares.

8 Mount each letter to the remaining red paper. Trim the excess, leaving a 1/16" matting around each letter.

9 Mount the word snow at the bottom right side of the blue square.

10 Randomly mount the snowflakes to the page. Cut and separate one to give the effect of going off the page.

11 Cut out around the snowmen on the remaining Snowmen square.

12 Using the foam dots, mount the snowmen above the word SNOW, slightly overlapping the edge of the folded frame.

Chapter 4

3-D and Home Decor

21. Coasters
page 55

22. Candle Skirts
page 56

23. Shadow Box
page 58

24. Wall Hanging
page 60

25. Place Setting Trio
page 62

26. Bronze Box
page 64

27. Heritage Frame
page 66

28. Ball Ornament
page 68

29. Pop-Up Ornament
page 70

30. Teardrop Ornament
page 72

Coasters

As inevitably as spring-cleaning, comes the welcome warmth of summer. There's no better way to celebrate than with a splash of fresh lemonade. Serve it on fruit-inspired Diamond Kite Coasters, and you're sure to get a smile. These coasters are made with the freshest of summer colors, and they're a perfect companion to any pool party, graduation party, or camping trip. If summer's not your thing, make your coasters in a holiday theme or in colors to match your home décor.

TECHNIQUE

Diamond Kite Fold

SUPPLIES

For folding
- 1 sheet Fruit paper[1]
- 1½" Scalloped Square punch[2]
- Liquid adhesive[3]

For project
- Coaster[4]
- 1 sheet green plaid paper (crop to 3 1/16" diameter circle)
- 1 sheet yellow paper (crop to 2 11/16" diameter circle)
- 1 sheet of red paper (crop to 2¾" diameter circle)
- Fun sun (glass with straw) stickers[5]
- Mounting tape
- Circle cutter or template
- Ruler, scissors or paper cutter

In this project: [1]NRN Designs, [2]Marvy® Uchida, [3]Delta, [4]M.C.G. Textiles, [5]Frances Meyer, copyright Cathy Heck Studio.

DIAMOND KITE FOLD

Punch eight squares of the fruit paper with the 1½" scalloped punch. Complete steps #1–#6 of the Diamond Fold (page 28) for each square, followed by:

1 Lift up the top flap on the left.

2 Press straight down on the crease, squishing the piece flat and creating a kite shape.

ASSEMBLY

1 Pick up piece #1 with the closed point at the bottom. Slightly open the two back flaps on the right side and place a small amount of adhesive in the crease.

2 With your other hand, pick up piece #2. Place the back left flap of piece #2 between the two flaps of piece

#1. The kite shape sits on top. Slide the pieces together until they stop and the bottom points meet.

3 Continue adding pieces in this manner.

4 After adhering piece #8, bring the flaps of piece #1 forward and into piece #8. There may be a small hole in the center. Add additional adhesive as necessary.

PROJECT ASSEMBLY

1 Mount the folded element centered on the yellow circle.

2 Mount the yellow circle centered on the red circle.

3 Mount the red circle centered on the green circle.

4 Peal and stick the glass sticker centered on the folded element.

5 Place the folded element into the coaster face down.

6 Peel and stick the cork backing to the coaster, sealing the folded element inside.

Candle Skirts

*T*ransform plain candleholders into striking centerpieces with candle skirts. This folded skirt allows you to choose from two different looks. Change the effects by switching the skirt from right side up to upside down. In this example, I have used a heart pattern paper. You can change the paper selection to suit your decorating needs. This skirt accommodates a 3/4" to 1" diameter taper candle.

TECHNIQUE
Three-Quarter Turnabout Fold

SUPPLIES
- 2 sheets Heart paper[1] (cut 15 2½" squares)
- Liquid adhesive[2]
- Ruler, pencil

In this project: [1]Folded Memories, [2]Delta.

2
Lay the next piece on top of the first, lining up the right folded edge of the first piece with the left folded edge of the second.

Keeping the edges together, slide the top piece down so that the bottom extends about ¼". Match the images so that the red line on the second piece hits the middle of the lower ribbon of the first piece.

3
Continue this process with all 15 pieces. The first piece will lie on top of the last to complete the pattern.

Note: Always use non-drip candles when using paper skirts. Never leave burning candles unattended. Paper candle skirts are NOT flame resistant or flame retardant.

THREE-QUARTER TURNABOUT FOLD

Before you begin, stack all the squares so that the heart image is right side up. Flip the stack over, to the right so the wrong side is facing up.

1
Fold the bottom edge up to the top. Fold all 15 pieces.

2
Stack all the pieces with the folded edge at the bottom. Using a ruler,

lightly mark ⅝" in from the right edge of each piece. The end of the green leaf on the folded edge is also a point of reference.

Complete the following steps for each piece:

3
Fold the lower left folded edge up and over to the right, pivoting on the marked point (⅝" in from the right). The new flap and the right edge should be parallel.

4
Using the same pivot point, fold the right side of the top flap over to the left to line up with the outside left edge.

ASSEMBLY

1
Place a small amount of adhesive on the lower right flap.

Use the back side of the element for an alternative pattern.

23

Shadow Box

TECHNIQUE
Standing Tulip

SUPPLIES

For folding
- 1 sheet 12" x 12" fuchsia/pink two-sided paper[1] (cut two 2½" squares; two 2¼" squares; two 1¾" squares)
- 1 sheet 8½" x 11" green paper (cut two 3¾" squares; two 3½" squares; two 2¾" squares; one 3½" x 3" rectangle)
- 1 sheet white paper
- Liquid adhesive[2]

For project
- 8" x 10" shadow box frame[3]
- 8" x 10" photo
- Adhesive[4]
- Boning tool
- Scissors

In this project: [1]Scrapbook Adventures, [2]Delta, [3]Keepsake Treasures, [4]Glue Dots.

The Standing Tulip can be created in virtually any size. Try using large squares to create life-size flowers or tiny squares to create dollhouse arrangements. In this project, the Standing Tulips draw out the flowers in the photo, creating a three-dimensional visual experience.

THE TULIP

Alternating the colors of the fuchsia/pink two-sided paper, complete steps #1–6 of the Diamond Fold (page 28) for each square, followed by:

1/8", depending on the size of the square you're using. Secure with adhesive.

1 Fold the side points of the top flaps in toward the middle about 1/4" to

2 Flip the piece over, and repeat step #1. Allow the pieces to dry before continuing.

3 Separate the open end, and place your finger inside. Push up on the bottom and out on the sides.

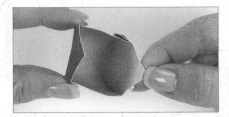

4 Curl the points out around your finger.

5 Using the point of the scissors, make a small hole in the bottom of the Tulip.

THE STEM

1 Fold the upper right corner down to the lower left corner to create a triangle.

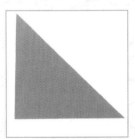

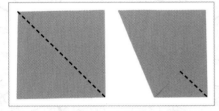

2 Open the piece flat. Fold the left edge up and over to the center crease.

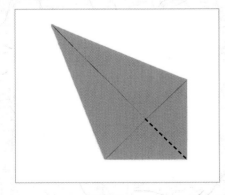

3 Fold the top edge down and over to the center crease.

4 Fold the bottom edge over to the center crease. A boning tool may be helpful here, due to the thickness of the paper layers.

5 Repeat step #4 with the right edge.

6 Fold the piece in half lengthwise to form a triangle.

7 Place a line of adhesive one third of the way up from the bottom to the top point.

8 Fold the triangle in half along the center crease line. Hold the piece

closed with a paperclip, if necessary. Allow the pieces to dry before continuing

9 Holding your piece by the glued edge, pull the point of the back piece down (like you're peeling a banana) to create the leaf.

ASSEMBLY

1 Place a generous amount of adhesive inside the Tulip over the small hole.

2 Choose the stem size according to the size of the flower. Insert the point of the stem into the small hole in the bottom of the Tulip.
Let dry completely before handling.

PROJECT ASSEMBLY

1 Prepare journaling or title information on the white paper.

2 Fold down ½" from the top of the green rectangle, and fold the remaining rectangle in half. It should stand like an easel.

3 Mount your journaling to the front of the green piece.

4 Mount your photo to the back of the shadow box.

5 Using Glue Dots, adhere the standing Tulips to the inside of the shadow box bottom. Arrange as desired.

6 Mount journaling in the center of the arrangement.

24

Wall Hanging

If you forgot to collect pinecones this year, or you're too busy to spend hours in a hobby store picking out the perfect arrangements for your Christmas wreath, don't worry. With a few simple folds, you can make a stylish wreath for any occasion. Add a few ribbons, and everyone will think you spent days putting it together.

TECHNIQUE
Envelope Wreath Fold

SUPPLIES
For folding
- 4 sheets 12" x 12" paper[1] (cut sixteen 6" squares)
- 7¼" circle template
- Liquid adhesive[2]

For project
- Artificial flowers[3]
- Floral wire
- Wired ribbon[4]
- Adhesive-backed picture hanger
- Ruler, scissors

In this project: [1]Anna Griffin Inc., [2]Delta, [3]Michaels®, [4]Horizon Fabrics.

ENVELOPE WREATH FOLD

Complete the following steps for each square:

1 With the wrong side of the square facing up, fold the top left corner down to the bottom right corner.

2 Stack all the triangle pieces. Lay the ruler in front of the stack at the folded edge, and mark the stack 5 1/2" in from the left.

3 Working with individual pieces, fold the left point over to the marked point.

4 Fold the point of the flap up to the left corner.

5 Lift the small flap straight up.

6 Press straight down on the crease, squishing it into a flat kite shape.

ASSEMBLY

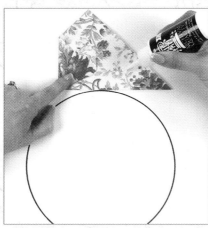

1 Working around a 7¼" circle template, lay the first piece down with the straight edge centered anywhere along the template. Place a small amount of adhesive in the center of the long flap.

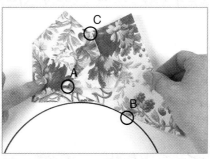

2 Lay the next piece on top of the first. Let the left edge of the kite on

piece #1 slide into the space behind the lower point of the kite of piece #2 about ½" (A). Angle the top piece so the bottom edge meets the circle template (B) and the top edges create a V shape (C).

3 Continue adding pieces in this manner, applying adhesive between each piece.

4 The first piece will sit on top of the last to complete the pattern.

PROJECT ASSEMBLY

1 Make bow loops with the wired ribbon.

2 Arrange the ribbon and flowers as desired. To wire them to the folded wreath, poke small holes through the paper and twist the wires at the back to secure.

3 On the back of the wreath, place the adhesive photo hanger at the top center.

Note: If a large circle template is hard to find, try a small plate. That's what I used!

25

Place Setting Trio

Add a special touch to your next gathering with personalized invitations, place cards, and matching napkin rings. In this example, three different looks were accomplished using the same fold while changing the paper size and pattern orientation. For more information on changing patterns, refer to the repetitive pattern section on page 10.

You can also change the look to suite your event. With the abundance of paper styles available, it should be a breeze to find paper to coordinate with almost any occasion.

TECHNIQUE

Two Step Fold

SUPPLIES

For folding
- 2 sheets Sunflower paper from Folded Memories (cut along the marked lines for 2½" squares)
- Liquid adhesive from Delta

For invitation
- Eight 2½" squares of Sunflower paper

For place card
- Eight inside squares of Sunflower paper

For napkin ring
- Eight inside squares of Sunflower paper

For project
- 2 sheets green cardstock
- 1 sheet marigold cardstock
- 1 sheet brown cardstock
- 1 sheet black cardstock
- 1 paper towel tube (cut into 1" lengths)
- Notched corner punch from Carl
- Stamp or computer generated message or names
- Mounting tape

Cropping specs for invitation
- Green: 5⅜" x 9⅝", fold in half; 4" diameter circle
- Black: 4⅝" x 5⅛"
- Marigold: 4½" x 5", punch each corner
- Brown: 3¾" diameter circle

Cropping specs for place card
- Brown: 6" x 5½", folded in half to 3" x 5½"
- Green: 5¼" x 2¾"
- Marigold: 5 "x 2"

Cropping specs for napkin ring
- Green: 1¼" x 6"

TWO STEP FOLD

Invitation

Place card

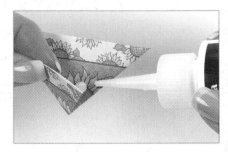

Napkin ring

The folding steps are the same for all three projects. They differ by size and pattern orientation. Here are the beginning pattern orientations for each project:

Complete steps #1 and #2 of the Two Step Variation Fold (page 50) with eight matching pieces, and assemble as follows.

ASSEMBLY

1 Hold the first piece with the folded edge at the bottom, and place a small amount of adhesive between the flaps, near the right edge.

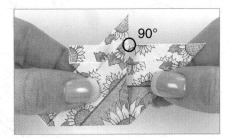

2 Slide the next piece in the space between the two flaps of the first piece. Line up the two pieces so that the bottom points meet and the top edges create a 90° angle. (For the napkin ring, slide the point down slightly to line up the image in the center.)

3 The third piece will line up so that the bottom point meets with the preceding piece and the inside edge sits next to the right edge of the first piece.

4 Continue adding pieces in this manner. The first piece will fit inside the last to complete the pattern.

CARD ASSEMBLY

1 Mount the black rectangle centered on the green card.

2 Mount the marigold rectangle centered on the black rectangle.

3 Mount the green circle centered ¼" down from the top of the marigold rectangle.

4 Mount the brown circle centered on the green circle.

5 Mount the folded element centered on the green circle.

6 Stamp your greeting.

PLACE CARD ASSEMBLY

1 Mount the green rectangle centered on the brown card.

2 Mount the marigold rectangle centered on the green rectangle.

3 Mount the folded element centered to the left on the marigold rectangle.

4 Stamp or write the name.

NAPKIN RING ASSEMBLY

1 Wrap the green strip around the paper towel tube section, and secure with tape.

2 Mount the folded element to the covered tube.

26

Bronze Box

TECHNIQUE
Square Box Fold

SUPPLIES

For folding
- 1 sheet bronze embossed paper[1] (cut two 10¾" squares)
- Liquid adhesive
- Boning tool
- Long ruler, 15" or greater
- Pencil, scissors

For project
- Skeleton leaves[2]
- ⅝" bronze ribbon[3]

In this project: [1]Black Ink, [2]Gold Leaf, [3]Morex Corp.

Give your next gift in a box they will want to keep. The Square Box Fold works best when made with stiff or heavy weight papers. Handmade papers and even wallpaper make good choices. My niece, Alisa, introduced me to this box fold, and I love its versatility. Whether for gift giving or decorating, this box is sure to get attention.

SQUARE BOX FOLD
Box bottom

1 Lay the ruler diagonally from point to point, and lightly mark along the center. Repeat from the opposite corners. When finished, there should be a light X in the center of the paper.

2 Fold all four of the corner points into the center mark.

3 Fold the lower edge up to the center. (Crease A)

4 Fold the upper edge down to the center. (Crease B)

5 Open the flaps flat, leaving the corner points in the center.

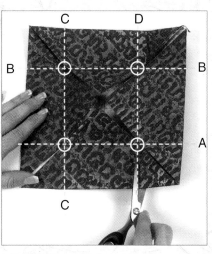

7 Cut the crease lines C and D, just to the intersections of crease lines A and B.

8 Open the upper and lower points to extend outward.

6 Repeat steps #3–5 with the opposite edges. (Creases C and D)

9 Stand the right and left edges up, allowing the small triangle points at each end to overlap.

10 Fold one point of the remaining two flaps up and over the side, pressing the triangle point into the center. Secure with adhesive.

11 Repeat step #10 with the remaining point.

Box lid
Repeat steps #1–10 with one exception; on step #3, fold all four corner points to within 1/16" of the center mark. This will create a slightly larger lid to fit over the box bottom.

PROJECT ASSEMBLY

1 Fill box as desired.

2 Place the lid on the box.

3 Tie the box with ribbon.

4 Top with gold skeleton leaves. Secure leaves with a small amount of adhesive.

27

Heritage Frame

TECHNIQUE
V Fold

SUPPLIES
For folding
- 26 pre-cut 4" doilies[1]
- Liquid adhesive[2]

For project
- One 12" x 12" sheet Marquina Marble Green paper[3] (crop to 8½" x 10½")
- 9¼" x 11¼" green matt board
- Mounting tape
- Oval cutter or template for 4¼" x 6¼" oval
- Sticky back easel

In this project: [1]Folded Memories, [2]Delta, [3]Scrap-Ease.

This beautiful frame, with the look of lace, is perfect for use with wedding or heritage photos. One of the interesting things about the V fold is that the same folded pieces that comprise the frame can also serve as decorative corner mounts. This project was created as a freestanding frame, but it could easily be adapted to fit a scrapbook page.

Note: Crease doilies gently; they can tear.

Complete the following steps for each doily half:

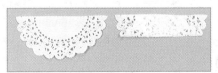

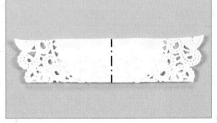

1 With the wrong side of the paper facing up and the straight edge at the top, fold the bottom up to the center of the straight edge.

2 Fold the piece in half from right to left to mark the center.

3 Open the piece flat so that the flap is in the back.

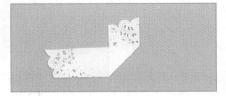

4 Fold the lower right edge up to the center crease.

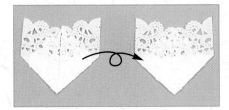

5 Repeat step #4 with the left side, and flip the piece over.

ASSEMBLY

1 Center the oval template or cutter on the Marquina Marble Green paper. Cut out and remove the oval. Place the first piece along the inside edge of the template, and place a small amount of glue toward the bottom right side of the edge of the piece.

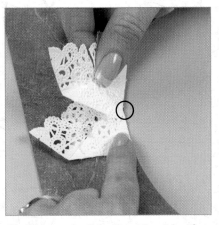

2 Start on the left along the side of the oval opening, and slide the lower point of each piece (about ¼") into the pocket created by the lace edge of the preceding piece.

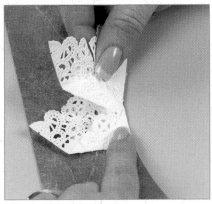

Line up the upper folded edge so that it lies along the center of the piece behind it.

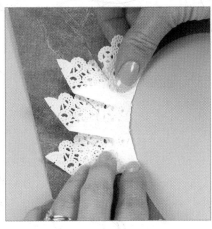

3 The outside edges should remain consistent. The amount of the point inside the pocket (along the inside edge) will vary as you work your way around the irregular opening. It will take 20-22 pieces to get around the oval.

4 The last piece slides behind the first to complete the pattern.

5 Use the remaining four folded pieces as corner mounts by sliding the corner of the paper into the pocket created by the lace edge. Part of the folded piece will lay behind the paper corner.

PAGE ASSEMBLY

1 Center your photo behind the frame and secure the frame to the photo with adhesive.

2 Center the frame and photo on the green matt board, and glue it down.

3 Attach the adhesive easel to the back of the matt board.

28

Ball Ornament

The ball ornament is an elegant addition to any Christmas tree. It can also be a creative gift for a special occasion. Make it in white, and give it away as part of a wedding gift. In blue or pink, it's perfect for a baby shower or as baby's first ornament (see page 22). Why should Christmas trees have all the fun? Make the ball ornament to match your home décor, incorporate it into your centerpieces, or hang it on a large plant in your living room.

TECHNIQUE

V Fold

SUPPLIES

For folding
- 45 pre-cut 4" doilies[1]

For project
- 3" foam[2] ball
- 3" square of white paper
- 1 box of straight pins
- 6 white ball-tip straight pins
- 24" of 1" wide white sheer wired ribbon
- 6" of ¼" wide white sheer ribbon
- 1 can of silver glitter spray[3]

In this project: [1]Folded Memories, [2]Plastifoam®, [3]Sherwin-Williams.

Complete steps #1–5 of the V fold on page 66, but don't flip over on step #5, followed by:

BALL ASSEMBLY

This assembly achieves a layered look by stacking the pieces in alternating rows as you work around the circumference of the ball. The assembly starts at the bottom of the ball and works up to the top.

1 Mold the white paper square to the Plastifoam ball, and secure with pins on the corners.

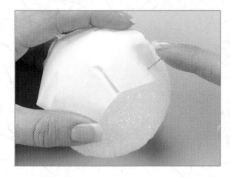

2 Place two folded pieces, point to point, on top of the paper square. Secure them with a pin at the outer points of each of the folded pieces.

3 Place two folded pieces, point to point, with the outside corners overlapping the previous pieces. All four points will meet in the center. Secure them with a pin at the outer points of each of the folded pieces. We'll call this the first row.

4 Start the second row by placing the point of the next piece 1/2" away from the center (where the four points of row one come together). Line the piece up so that it falls between two of the pieces of the first row.

5 Continue adding pieces to the second row, overlapping the first row.

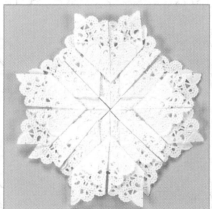

6 The third row will lay 1/2" up from the second row. Alternate the points with the second row, while lining up the third row with the points from the first row. Here is a flat view to help illustrate the process.

7 Continue in the same manner, alternating rows as you move toward the top. Near the widest point of the ball, the outside edges of the folded pieces won't touch each other.

8 As you near the top of the ball, the outer edges of the pieces will begin to overlap. To avoid pins showing, place the pins further back and in from the edges.

9 The last two pieces will cover the ball. The pins will be showing.

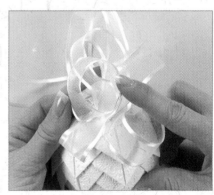

10 Make bow loops with the wide ribbon, and pin the ribbon into the top of the ball. Use the white tipped pins to blend into the ball. This will cover the pins left showing in step #9.

11 Make a loop with the narrow ribbon, and pin it at the center of the top of the ball.

12 Lightly spray the ball ornament with glitter. Hang and enjoy.

29

Pop-Up Ornament

*T*his pop-up ornament is great for sending through the mail or convenient year-to-year storage. When flat, this ornament looks like a clever little card or small book, but hidden inside is a three-dimensional star just waiting to pop out.

TECHNIQUE
Diamond Fold

SUPPLIES
For folding
- 1 sheet red-with-gold-stars vellum[1] (cut five 3½" squares)

For project
- Adhesive[2]
- 1 sheet red heavy-weight cardstock (cut two 1¾" squares)
- 8" red ⅛" ribbon (cut in half)
- Star stamp[3]
- Pigment ink[4]
- Embossing powder

In this project: [1]The Paper Co., [2]Glue Dots, [3]Close to My Heart®, [4]Color Box.

Note: Vellum can be tricky to adhere. Liquid adhesives can cause it to warp and tapes to show through. I found that the Glue Dots work best.

DIAMOND FOLD

Follow steps #1–6 of the Diamond Fold from page 28, followed by:

POP-UP ASSEMBLY

Before you begin: Stamp and emboss the cardstock squares. Be sure all diamond pieces have the closed point at the bottom.

1 Place Glue Dots just in from the edge at each of the four corners.

2 Lay the next diamond piece directly on top of the first, carefully lining up all points.

3 Continue in this manner with all pieces, stacking one on top of another.

4 Place Glue Dots on top of the last piece; place one of the lengths of ribbon extending from the top point.

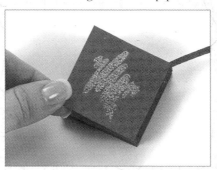

5 Top off the stack with one of the cardstock squares.

6 Flip the stack over and repeat steps #4 and #5.

TO POP-UP

1 Pull the front and back covers around to be back-to-back.

2 Tie the ribbons at the top.

30

Teardrop Ornament

This beautiful ornament fold was taught to me by a 10-year-old boy named Kevin Vielle. Kevin explained to me that it is his family's tradition to make these ornaments at Christmas time and fill them with treats. The ornaments would be hung on the tree, and on Christmas the children would open the ornaments and enjoy the long-awaited goodies. Depending on the size of ornament, I think it would make an excellent place for a secret gift for someone special.

SUPPLIES

- 6" square of Blue with gold embossed cardstock[1]
- Adhesive
- Gold ribbon

In this project: [1]Robin's Nest Press.

TEARDROP ORNAMENT FOLD

Complete steps #1–5 of the Diamond Fold (page 28), followed by:

1 Open the piece flat and rotate to look like a diamond, with the wrong side facing up.

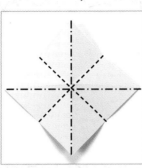

2 Fold the upper left edge down to the center crease line.

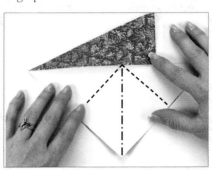

3 Repeat step#2 with the bottom left edge.

4 Open the piece flat, repeat steps #2 and #3 from all four corners.

The crease configuration should look like the lines on the example.

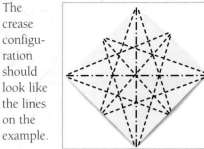

5 Press up and in on the center edges of all four sides, creating a star shape.

6 Pull all four points up to meet each other. You may have to push the center down to allow the outer points to come up.

7 Secure the ribbon with adhesive inside the points at the top.

Chapter **5**

For Kids

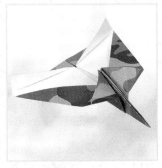

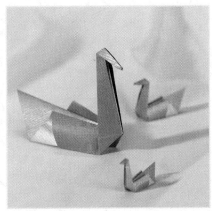

31. Bug Box
page 74

32. Silver and Gold Birds
page 76

33. Airplane
page 78

34. Airplane Variation
page 80

35. Bats
page 82

36. Pencil Pinwheels
page 84

37. Stamped Birthday Card
page 86

38. Cootie Catchers
page 88

39. "Best Buds" Frame
page 90

40. Necklace & Bracelet
page 92

Bug Box

This simple box is great for stashing treasures or for gift giving. By changing the paper or decoration, you can dress it up or down. This box can be made from any size or type of paper. Have fun experimenting with the different shapes and styles you can make. The Bug Box was created with the help of my kids, Garrett (7) and Marissa (6), who fingerprinted white paper to look like bugs.

TECHNIQUE
Rectangular Box Fold

SUPPLIES
- Kid's fingers
- 2 sheets 8½" x 11" white cardstock
- Colored inkpads
- Black marker
- Long ruler or yardstick
- Pencil, clear tape

Preparing the Paper

Use brightly colored inks to fingerprint your paper. Be sure to change the direction and size of the fingerprints. You can combine fingerprints to get the look of heads and bodies. To create long bodies for dragonflies or butterflies, imprint your entire finger. Experiment on scratch paper to determine the combinations that you like best. Have fun using a black marker to add defining details like eyes, wings, and antennas.

Box bottom

1 With the wrong side of the fingerprint bug paper facing up, fold the long edges in ½". This step will help reinforce the sides of your box.

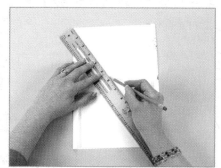

2 Place a long ruler or yardstick diagonally from corner to corner. Mark along the center with a light pencil line. Repeat using opposite corners. When you're finished, there should be a light X in the center of the paper.

3 Fold the short edge in to the center point and crease well. Repeat with the opposite end.

4 Open the paper flat. Fold the long edge into the center mark and crease well. Repeat with the opposite edge. Leave it folded.

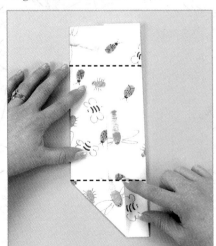

5 Choose any corner. Fold it across toward the center to meet the crease line, creating a triangle.

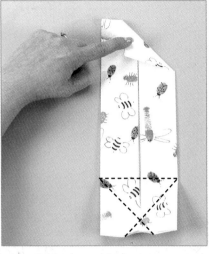

6 Unfold the triangle, and repeat step #7 on each of the remaining corners.

7 Lift up the long edges, and tuck in the triangle section to create the corners of the box.

8 Fold the flap, which extends beyond the height of the long edge, over into the box and tape it down.

9 Repeat steps #9 and #10 on the opposite end.

Box lid

Follow the steps for the box bottom with one exception. On steps #3 and #5, don't fold the edges all the way to the center X. Fold the edges to approximately ⅛" away from the center mark. This will make the lid slightly larger, so the bottom will easily fit inside.

32

Silver and gold Birds

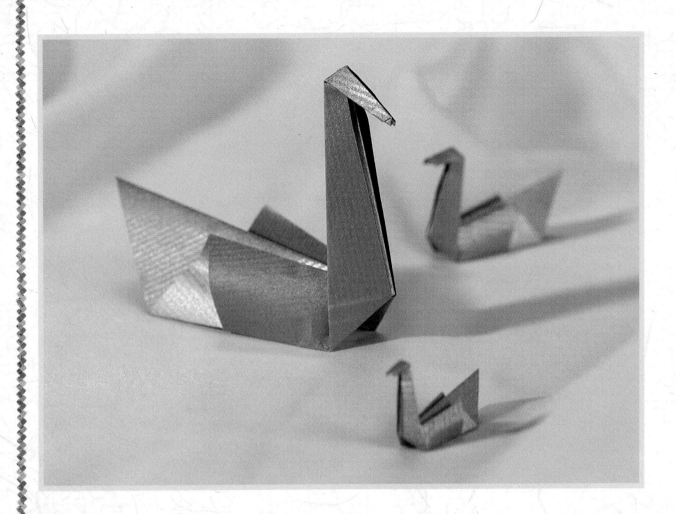

*T*his Basic Bird is as versatile as it is fun to make. These birds can be folded in nearly any size and color and be put to use a number of ways. Make a special birthday card by mounting a bird to cardstock with the caption "a little birdie told me it's your birthday" or string several different color and size birds with fishing line to make a colorful mobile. What about wearable art? Add an adhesive-back pin and your bird becomes a fashion statement.

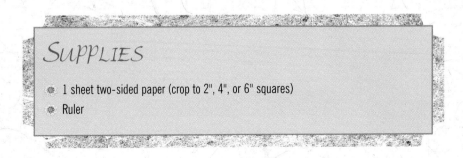

SUPPLIES

- 1 sheet two-sided paper (crop to 2", 4", or 6" squares)
- Ruler

Basic Bird Fold

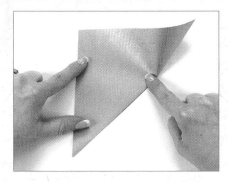

1 Fold the bottom right corner up to the top left corner.

2 Open the piece flat and rotate to a diamond shape (crease running horizontally through the middle).

3 Fold the left point in approximately ½" (slightly less for 1½" or 2" squares).

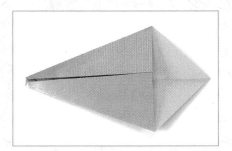

4 Fold the bottom left and top left edges in to the center crease.

5 Flip the piece over. Repeat step #4.

6 Fold the left point over to the right, stopping about ¾" from the right point.

7 Fold the small point back to the left about ¾".

9 Hold the bird by the bottom edge, pull up on the top flap to extend the neck about 90°, and crease the bottom of the neck.

8 Fold the piece in half along the center crease.

10 Adjust the angle of the head by gently pulling up on the small flap. Crease to hold the head in place.

33

Airplane

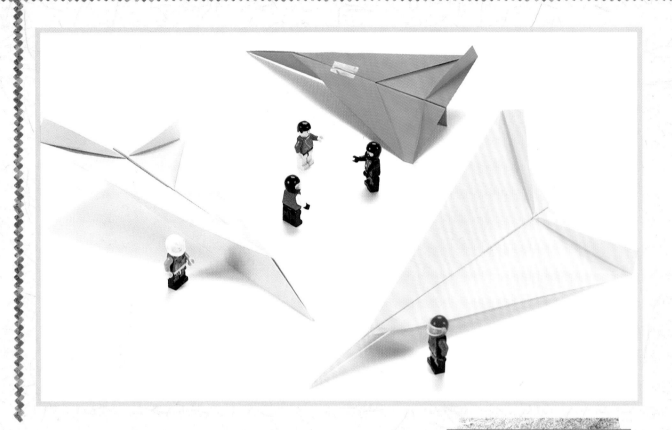

Need something to do? How about airplane races? Grab a partner and make a few planes. Decorate them so you can tell them apart, and then let them fly. Try different techniques for distance, or see if you can make your plane do tricks. Have fun!

SUPPLIES

- 8½" x 11" sheet lightweight paper
- Ruler, clear tape

Airplane
With this fold, it is important to crease well at each step.

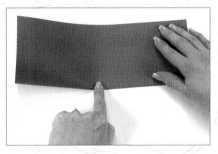

1 Working with your paper's long edges at the top and bottom, fold the bottom edge up to the top.

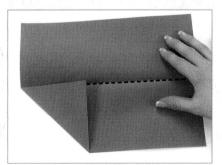

2 Open the piece flat, fold the lower left corner up and over to the center crease.

3 Fold the upper left corner down and over to the center crease.

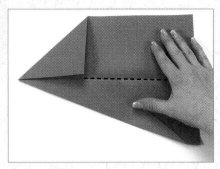

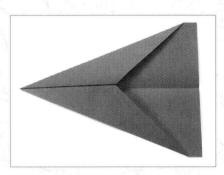

4 Fold the bottom diagonal edge up to the center crease.

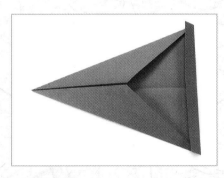

5 Fold the top diagonal edge down to the center crease.

6 Fold the right side edge over to the left about ¾". (Call this the rear flaps.)

7 Fold the bottom edge up to the top along the center crease line.

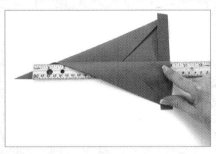

8 Lay your ruler on top of the plane along the bottom edge. Fold the top flap down over the ruler. Remove the ruler, and crease.

9 Flip the plane over. Repeat steps #8 and #9.

10 Lay the plane flat. Place a small strip of tape over the center crease line, near the middle of the plane.

11 Fold the rear flaps out from the center crease to the outside edge, creating long triangles.

12 Hold the plane upright. Adjust the rear flaps to stand up.

13 FLY!

Option: *Have fun coloring your airplane to give it your own personal look.*

34

Airplane Variation

*T*ry this suped up model of a paper airplane. Making a few changes to the Airplane on page 78 gives the Variation model a totally different look. I recommend that you try the previous Airplane model before moving on to this one.

Airplane Variation

This model will be thick in places. Be sure to crease well. Complete steps #1–6 of the Airplane (page 78), followed by:

1 Fold the plane in half so that the nose extends from the center of the rear ¾".

2 Notice the long triangle sections extending from behind the flap on either side.

With your left hand place your finger and thumb on each side of the flap at the point where it meets the triangle sections.

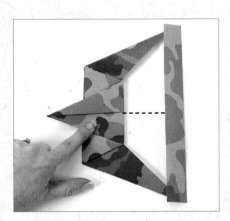

3 Fold the nose point back to the left, creasing at the point where your fingers were placed.

4 Fold the plane in half along the center crease.

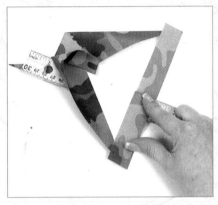

5 Lay your ruler on top of the plane along the bottom edge. Fold the top flap down over the ruler.

6 Remove the ruler, and crease the lower edge only. Allow the inside flap to remain upright.

7 Flip the plane over. Repeat steps #6 and #7.

8 Open the wings flat. Fold the rear flaps out from the center crease to the outside edge, creating long triangles.

9 Hold the plane upright. Adjust the rear flaps to stand up.

10 Slide a paper clip onto the center flaps below the crease line.

11 Slide a paper clip onto the rear of the plane below the crease line.

35

Bats

Folded bats are a Halloween favorite. These bats can be made in any size. Add them to your Halloween décor by hanging them from fishing line to look as though they're in flight. These bats make great finger puppets or party favors.

SUPPLIES

For folding
- Black paper cropped to a 5" square

For project
- Fishing line
- Scissors, ruler, clear tape

Bat Fold

Begin with steps #1-6 of the Triangle fold (page 18), followed by:

1 With the closed point at the bottom, fold the top left flap over to the right. There will be three flaps on one side and one flap on the other side.

2 Fold the bottom edge of the top right flap up and over to the center crease.

3 Slide your finger between the two back flaps on the right. Push the top flaps over to the left.

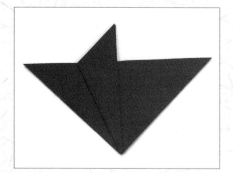

4 Fold the bottom edge of the top left flap up and over to the center crease.

5 Fold the top left flap back over to the right side.

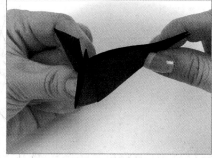

6 Pick the piece up and pull the two remaining full flaps together in the back.

7 Use the scissors to cut two soft C shapes along the open edges of the flaps. This gives detail to the wings.

8 Place the piece flat with the full flaps on each side. Use scissors to make a snip ½" long, starting about ¼" out from the center point on each side.

9 Fold the cut center point up.

10 Turn the piece around, and *voilà* a bat!

11 Embellish the bat with eyes, if you like.

Assembly

Tape a length of fishing line to the back of the bat for hanging.

36

Pencil Pinwheels

SUPPLIES

For folding

- 1 sheet colored paper (crop to 3" square; save the remainder)
- 1 sheet a contrasting-color paper (crop to 3" square; save the remainder)

For project

- Flower punch[1] (as an alternative to the punch, you can trace around a nickel and cut it out)
- Map pin or tack
- Mounting tape, pencil, clear tape, ruler, decorative scissors, scissors

In this project: [1]Family Treasures.

*J*azz up your pencils with these colorful pinwheels. Pinwheels work well with any paper you might have laying around. If you don't have your own paper stash, look around the house for computer paper, construction paper, newspaper, or even pages out of a magazine to use. Because this project uses pins, please ask an adult for help.

Pinwheel

1 Decide which color will be the outside and which will be on the inside of your pinwheel. *Optional: With the decorative scissors, trim around the outer edges of the square you have chosen for the inside of the pinwheel.*

2 Using a piece of mounting tape in the center, attach the inside square to the outside square.

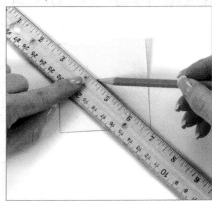

3 Place the ruler diagonally from corner to corner. Make a light pencil line from point to point.

4 Repeat using opposite corners. When you're finished, there should be a light X on the paper.

5 Cut along the pencil lines from each corner in toward the center. Stop about ¾" from the center.

6 Punch a flower from a scrap of the inside colored paper.

Assembly

Have an adult help you with the assembly.

1 Reinforce every other point of the square with a small piece of clear tape.

2 Push the map pin through the center of the punched flower.

3 Beginning with any one of the reinforced points, fold, but don't crease, the point in toward the center mark.

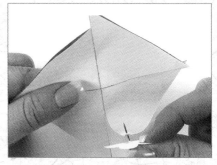

4 Push the map pin with the flower through the point as close to the end as possible.

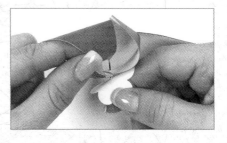

5 Repeat steps #3 and #4 with the remaining three reinforced points.

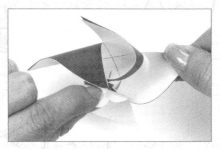

6 Push the map pin through the center of the "X."

7 Push the map pin into the eraser of the pencil. Push the pin in as far as possible without the point coming out the other side.

37

Stamped Birthday Card

My kids like to stamp, color, and fold. This project combines all three in one fun card. Create your own patterned paper by stamping and coloring a square shape stamp. I used a happy birthday stamp; you can use whatever you'd like to fit the occasion. Cards are not the only things you can make with your folded element. Use it to decorate a gift bag, top off a package, or hang it from a ribbon to use as an ornament.

TECHNIQUE
Single Flap Fold

SUPPLIES

For folding
- 12 sheets light-weight white paper
- Happy Birthday stamp[1] and ink
- Liquid adhesive[2]
- Scissors, colored pencils

For card
- 1 sheet blue cardstock cropped to: 8½" x 5½" and folded in half
- 1 sheet yellow cardstock cropped to: 4¼" square
- 1 sheet green cardstock cropped to: 3¾" square
- 1 sheet red cardstock cropped to: 3½" square
- Mounting tape

In this project: [1]Close to My Heart, [2]Delta.

Single Flap Fold

Prepare by stamping, coloring, and cutting out eight squares. Turn all squares so that the "happy" is at the top. Flip the stack over, to the right. Now the "happy" should be at the top with the wrong side of the paper facing up.

Complete the following steps for each square:

1 Fold the top right corner down to the bottom left corner.

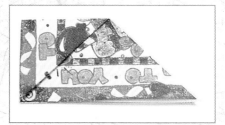

2 Fold the top left point down to the bottom left corner.

Assembly

1 Place a small amount of adhesive in the middle of the right side of the piece.

2 Lay the next piece on top of the first. Line up the top folded edge of the second piece with the inside folded edge of the first piece. The two pieces will make a straight line at the top.

3 Continue adding pieces in the same way

4 When you get to the last few pieces, you'll need to slide the long point under the first piece to continue.

5 The last piece goes on top of the seventh piece and behind the first piece to complete the pattern.

Card Assembly

1 Center the red square on the green square and tape it down.

2 Center the green square on the yellow square and tape it down.

3 Center the folded element on the red square and tape it down.

4 Center the squares and folded element on the card, like a diamond (the points will hang off the edges), tape them down.

5 Cut the points of the squares off at the edges of the card.

38

Cootie Catchers

This fun folded plaything has been around for ages. There are not many grown-ups that wouldn't recognize one. The markings and phrases may have changed, but the base remains the same. Cootie Catchers are especially popular with school age kids. They seem to have as much fun decorating them as playing with them.

Cootie Catchers make great party favors. Make one for each child from a solid color paper. Place them on the party table upside down and fill them with candy and other party favors. When the party is under way and most of the goodies have been consumed, decorate the Cootie Catchers as your party craft project.

Supplies

For folding
- Square paper (5" or larger is recommended)

For project
- Markers or crayons

Cootie Catcher

1 Fold the bottom edge up to the top edge, making a rectangle.

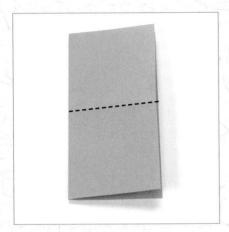

2 Open the piece flat. Fold the left side over to the right.

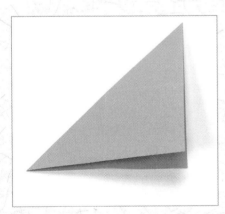

3 Open the piece flat. Flip the paper over. Fold the upper left corner down to the lower right corner to form a triangle.

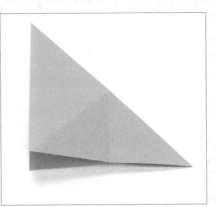

4 Open the piece flat. Fold upper right corner down to the lower left corner.

5 Fold each of the four corners into the center.

6 Flip the piece over. Repeat step #5.

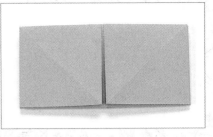

7 Fold the bottom edge up to the top

8 With both hands, grasp the bottom folded edge of the piece. Bring both thumbs toward the center, forming a layered diamond shape.

9 Slide a finger or thumb under each of the outside flaps to pop them out.

39

"Best Buds" Frame

"Best Buds"

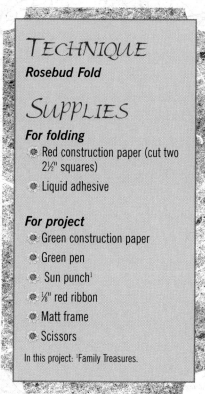

TECHNIQUE
Rosebud Fold

SUPPLIES

For folding
- Red construction paper (cut two 2½" squares)
- Liquid adhesive

For project
- Green construction paper
- Green pen
- Sun punch[1]
- ⅛" red ribbon
- Matt frame
- Scissors

In this project: [1]Family Treasures.

Nothing makes me smile quite like pictures of friends. This custom frame is a great way to display photos of your "best bud." These folded rosebuds are easy to make and can be arranged in many different ways to suit your decorating style. Real roses come in a variety of colors, so don't feel limited to using red for your project. Use the colors you like best or the ones that compliment the photo you plan to display.

Rosebud Fold

Complete the following steps for each square:

1 Cut the squares in half on the diagonal to create four triangles.

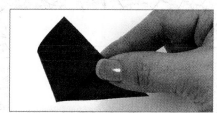

2 With the long edge of the triangle at the bottom, bring the left point over to the right to the middle of the right side. Don't crease.

3 Bring the right point over to the middle of the left side.

4 Fold the top triangle point to the back.

5 Flip the piece over, so the triangle is pointing down.

6 Fold the top left point down to meet the point of the triangle.

7 Fold the top right point down to meet the triangle point. Glue all layers down.

8 Flip the piece over.

Assembly

1 Punch two sun shapes out of the green paper.

2 Cut each sun in half.

3 With the straight edge at the bottom, wrap the green punch around the bottom of the rosebud, and glue from behind.

Project Assembly

1 Cut four long narrow strips that gently curve toward the top out of the green paper.

2 Cut six or seven leaves out of the green paper. The leaves should be about 1" long, and they don't all have to be the same shape. Rose leaves are jagged on the edges, so don't be too perfect.

3 Use a green pen to draw a curved line down the center of each leaf. This makes them look as if they're bending.

4 Arrange the stems at different lengths, like a bouquet, and glue them to each other in the center.

5 Glue the stems to the side of the matt frame.

6 Arrange the rosebuds and leaves on the stems as you like, and glue them down.

7 Tie a bow with the red ribbon, and glue it to the bouquet where the stems come together.

8 Write your name or a saying like "best buds" at the bottom of the frame. There are many alphabet templates available if you want a professional look.

Hannah in yellow. Here is another option for your folded rosebuds. Draw from colors in the photo to determine the color of the roses.

40

Necklace & Bracelet

TECHNIQUE

Interlocking Chain Fold

SUPPLIES

For folding

- 2 sheets yellow computer paper (cut 20 rectangles 1½" x 4")
- 2 sheets lime green computer paper (cut 22 rectangles 1½" x 4")
- 3 sheets blue computer paper (cut 42 rectangles 1½" x 4")

For projects

- 6" ribbon or yarn in a matching color

Interlocking chain necklaces and bracelets can be created with just about any light-weight paper. When I was a kid, we made them out of gum wrappers. The necklace can take as many as seventy pieces, depending on the size you use. I admit that seventy pieces is a lot, so keep this project in mind for long car rides or a rainy day activity. Some kids like to make continuous chains, competing with their friends to see whose will be the longest over a given period of time. The sky is the limit. Experiment with papers and colors to see how many different looks you can come up with.

Interlocking Chain

Complete the following steps for each rectangle:

1 With the long edges at the top and bottom, fold the bottom edge up to the top.

2 Open the piece flat. Fold the bottom edge up to the center crease line.

3 Fold the top edge down to the center crease line.

4 Fold the piece in half along the center crease line.

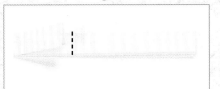

5 Fold left end over to the right to mark the center, and then return the left end to the left side.

6 Fold the left end into the center.

7 Fold the right end into the center.

8 Fold the piece in half at the center mark. We'll call the open end "the legs."

Assembly

For the necklace

You'll need: 33 blue pieces, 17 green pieces, and 16 yellow pieces.

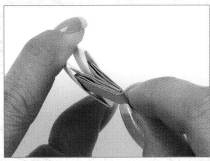

1 Hold one piece with the legs at the top. Working from the right, slide the legs of the next piece in at the top between the inside and outside flaps of each leg of the first piece.

2 Push the piece in until it stops.

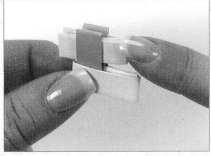

3 Turn the pieces over so that the last piece added will have the legs at the top (looks like the letter "L"). Continue adding pieces, alternating the colors yellow and green after each blue piece.

4 Thread the ribbon through the ends of the first and last piece, and secure with a bow or knot.

For the bracelet

You'll need: 9 blue pieces, 5 green pieces, and 4 yellow pieces.

Follow the same steps as for the necklace.

Resource guide

The projects in this book were made with products from the following companies:

Accu-Cut
1053 E. Dodge
PO Box 1053
Freemont, NE 68025
800-288-1670
www.accucut.com

All Night Media/Plaid
3225 Westech Dr
Norcross, GA 30092
687-291-8100
www.allnightmedia.com

Anna Griffin Inc.
733 Lambert Dr.
Atlanta, GA 30324
404-817-8170
www.annagriffin.com

Berwick
9th & Bomboy lane
PO Box 428
Berwick, PA 18603
570-759-7290
www.berwickindustries.com

Black Ink Papers/Graphic Products
Corp
455 Maple Ave
Carpentersville, IL 60110
800-323-1658

Carl Manufacturing
1862 S. Elmhurst Rd
Mt. Prospect, IL 60056
800-257-4771
www.carl-products.com

Carolees Creations
1350 W 5000 N
Smithfield, UT 84335
435-563-9336
www.caroleescreations.com

Cathy Heck Studio
3403 Mountain Top Circle
Austin, TX 78731
512-467-7681

Close To My Heart
1199 West 700 S
Pleasant Grove, UT 84062
888-655-6552
Southern CA area
909-776-1906
www.closetomyheart.com

Cock-a-Doodle Design
3759 W 2340 S suite D
Salt Lake City, UT 84120
www.cockadoodledesign.com

Creating Keepsakes
14901 Heritagecrest Way
Bluffdale, UT 84065
801-984-2070
www.creatingkeepsakes.com

Daisy D's Paper
1690 No 400 E
No Ogden, UT 84414
801-737-9152

Delta Technical Coatings
2550 Pellissier Pl
Whittier, CA 90601
800-423-1435
www.deltacrafts.com

Design Originals
2425 Cullen St
Fort Worth, TX 76107
817-877-0067
www.d-originals.com

EK Success Ltd
PO Box 1141, 125 Entin Rd
Clifton, NJ 07014
973-458-0540
www.eksuccess.com

Family Treasures
24922 Anza Dr unit D
Valencia CA 91335
800-413-2645
www.familytreasures.com

Fiskars
7811 W. Stewart Ave.
Wausau, WI 54401
715-842-2091
www.fiskars.com

Folded Memories
23632 Hwy 99 #F135
Edmonds WA 98026
425-673-7422
www.foldedmemories.com

Frances Meyer
PO Box 3088
Savannah, GA 31402
912-748-5252
www.francesmeyer.com

Galaxy Markers/American Crafts
PO Box 512
Orem, UT 84059
www.ultimatepens.com

Glue Dots
5575 S. Westridge Dr
New Berlin, WI 53150
262-814-8500
www.gluedots.com

Gold Leaf
PO Box 458
Brisbane, CA 94005
650-588-8886
www.gold-leaf.com

Hunt Corporation
121 Anna Drive
Statesville, NC 28625
1-800-TRY-HUNT
www.hunt-corp.com

It Takes Two
100 Minnesota Ave
Le Sueur, MN 56058
507-665-6271
www.ittakestwo.com

Klutz
455 Portage Ave
Palo Alto, CA 94306-2213
800-737-4123
www.klutz.com

Kolubki Trading Co
Products available through
Fascinating folds
www.fascinating-folds.com

M.C.G. Textiles
13845 Magnolia Ave
Chino CA 91710
800-856-2499

MM Colors by Design
7723 Densmore Ave
Van Nuys, CA 91436
800-832-8436
www.colorsbydesign.com

Making Memories
PO Box 1188
Centerville, UT 84014
801-294-0430
www.makingmemories.com

Marvy Uchida
3535 Del Amo Blvd
Torrance, CA 90503
310-793-2200
www.uchida.com

Morex Corp
220 N Belvidere Ave 2nd floor
PO Box 7577
York, PA 17404
717-852-7771
www.morexcorp.com

NRN Designs
5142 Argosy
Huntington Beach, CA 92649
714-898-6363
www.nrndesigns.com

The Paper Co.
205 Chubb Ave
Lyndherst, NJ 07071
800-525-3196
www.anwcrestwood.com

The Paper Patch
PO Box 414
Riverton, UT 84065
801-253-3018
www.paperpatch.com

Plastifoam/Syndicate Sales
2025 N Wabash St, PO Box 756
Kokomo, IN 46903
800-428-0515
www.syndicatesales.com

Robins Nest Press
1179 North 3000 West
Vernal, UT 84078
435-789-5387
www.robinsnest-scrapbook.com

Scrapbook Adventures/Rocky
Mountain Scrapbook Co.
526 N.675 E
Pleasant Grove, UT 84042
801-785-5387

Scrap-Ease/What's New Ltd
3716 E Main St
Mesa, AZ 85205
480-830-4581
www.whatsnewltd.com

Sherwin-Williams
www.sherwinwilliams.com

Stampa Rosa
60 Maxwell Court
Santa Rosa, CA 95401
707-570-0763
www.stamparosa.com

Looking for paper folding products on line? Here are a few of my favorite sites:

www.foldedmemories.com

www.fascinating-folds.com

www.stamporium.com

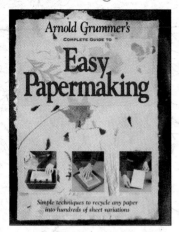
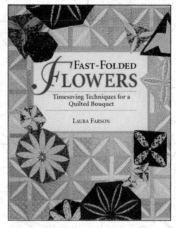

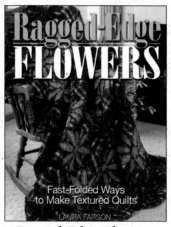